IMPROVISING
Jazz Piano.

Amsco Publications
New York/London/Sydney/Cologne

Edited by Ronnie Ball
Cover design by Pearce Marchbank
Cover photography by Gered Mankowitz
Book design and music engraving by W.R. Music Service

Order No. AM 32483
US International Standard Book Number: 0.8256.2256.5
UK International Standard Book Number: 0.7119.0191.0

Exclusive Distributors:
Music Sales Corporation
225 Park Avenue South, New York, NY 10003
Music Sales Limited
8/9 Frith Street, London W1V 5TZ England
Music Sales Pty. Limited
120 Rothschild Street, Rosebery, Sydney, NSW 2018, Australia

Printed in the United States of America by
Vicks Lithograph and Printing Corporation

This book is being published posthumously and is dedicated to its author, who died on April 3, 1984. The following is an excerpt from the memorial service held shortly after his death.

John Mehegan was my friend. He's not here today to laugh with us, to cry with us, to play with us — and that leaves a very big empty place in our lives. He deeply touched my life and those of my entire family. We feel privileged and very grateful for that.

I'd like to share with you some of my recollections of this brilliant, complex, truly unique man.

One of the things John was most proud of was his Irish heritage. He loved being the son of a blacksmith. He was born John Francis Mehegan, to John James Mehegan, blacksmith, and Mary Louise Mehegan, a church singer. A twin brother died at birth and John grew up as an only child in the Wethersfield-Hartford area of Connecticut. He left Wethersfield as a very young man, moved to New York and pursued his career in music.

A true Gemini, a man of opposites, a man of extremes, he always championed the underdog. (Even at the race track — he played the long shots.) He worked hard, played hard, loved intensely, hated with a vengeance, was tender to the tiniest animal, and challenged the biggest man. Proud of his peasant background, he enjoyed mingling with the elite. He was at home in a funky bar or in an elegant continental restaurant.

He belonged to no one but himself and yet he belonged to everyone. He had that very rare gift that made each person he touched seem to be the most important person in the world. It's a quality that must have been very difficult for his loved ones to endure, but it was a part of his greatness — as a performer, a teacher, and a man.

John had a *joie de vivre* and a commitment to life — a tremendous energy and drive. He was open to all that life offered and he gave back ten-fold. He struggled to see things with an overview free of ethnic or religious orientation. He loved geography, history, horses, books, words, movies — especially old ones — and, of course, baseball. He was a trivia buff and loved to take on a challenge in that arena.

There was a relentless quality in John — a sense of how important a commodity time is — how limited our allotment is. He loved clocks and watches. There was an urgency in the way he saw through the cutting of the record he had promised to do. On the day after he completed it, he had a heart attack.

He then approached completing the revision of his book, Jazz Improvisation, and the writing of a new book (this book), with the same relentless drive and urgency. Both projects were finished before this recent illness. It was almost as if he knew. Yet, he always worked that way.

In his own words, he was a "survivor." He often used the word "dinosaur" when referring to himself. He had a marvelous sense of humor — a beautiful laugh, as his daughter, Tara, once pointed out. A man of wit, charm, talent and intelligence was John. But one cannot overlook his anger, his lament for all the injustice, the cruelty, the insensitivity and the pain he saw in our world.

Life often seemed like one big, long, financial struggle for John, yet his focus, his life force was so strong in other areas that it simply couldn't crush him. It never seemed to matter that much in the final analysis. Anyway, his legacy to us cannot be measured by money. He left as his estate a great gift to the world — his books, his records, his music, his love.

It seems right that after a career of fifty years and a very full personal life; that after all his travels of the world, of the mind, of the spirit; it seems right that he should end up back here in Connecticut. His ashes will be buried at Willowbrook Cemetery, Section Eleven, on Weston Road in Westport.

Well, John, what more is there to say? "There'll Never Be Another You." Your family, your friends, your students, your colleagues, your fans and a whole generation of musicians know that you were here. Your brilliance shone for awhile on all of us — in twelve keys. Some of the sunshine has gone away.

Lucille King
Weston, Connecticut
April 1984

Chapter 1

The Harmonic Vocabulary (Introduction)

The principle of jazz improvisation involves the abandoning of the melody and the creating of new ideas from the resources of the harmony (chord changes) of a tune, arpeggios, modes, ornamental tones, etc. Because of this, it is essential that the student have a clear and concise idea of the use of harmony in dealing with jazz improvisation.

The diatonic system dating back to the 17th Century forms the basis for the jazz harmonic vocabulary. The diatonic system divides into two sub-systems, the triad system and the seventh chord system.

The Triad System:

The student is advised to be very familiar with the twelve major scales and, at least, the twelve harmonic minor scales before proceeding with this text.

Lesson: Play the scale-tone triads of Fig. 1 through Fig. 13 in both hands, with the left hand in the octave immediately below the right hand, until they can be played automatically from memory in any key.

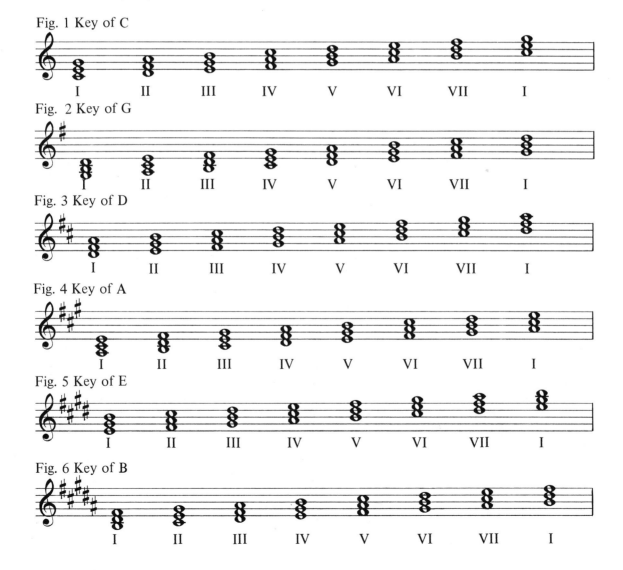

Fig. 1 Key of C

Fig. 2 Key of G

Fig. 3 Key of D

Fig. 4 Key of A

Fig. 5 Key of E

Fig. 6 Key of B

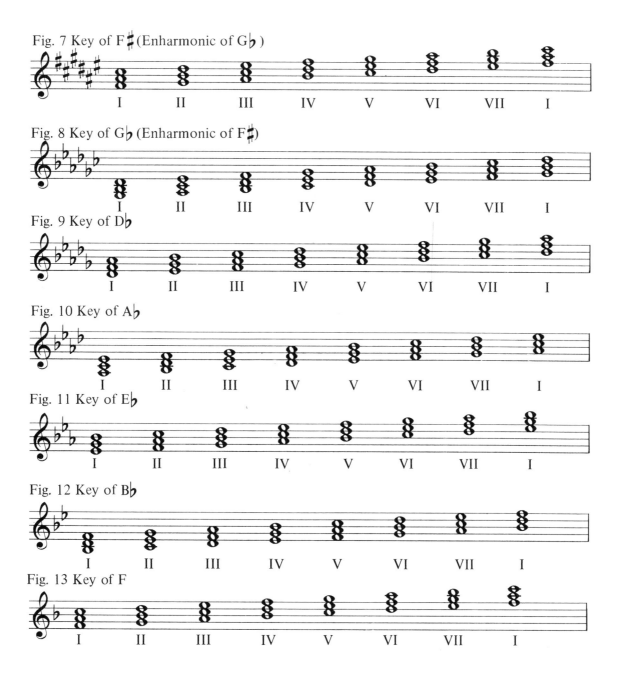

Fig. 7 Key of F♯ (Enharmonic of G♭)

I   II   III   IV   V   VI   VII   I

Fig. 8 Key of G♭ (Enharmonic of F♯)

I   II   III   IV   V   VI   VII   I

Fig. 9 Key of D♭

I   II   III   IV   V   VI   VII   I

Fig. 10 Key of A♭

I   II   III   IV   V   VI   VII   I

Fig. 11 Key of E♭

I   II   III   IV   V   VI   VII   I

Fig. 12 Key of B♭

I   II   III   IV   V   VI   VII   I

Fig. 13 Key of F

I   II   III   IV   V   VI   VII   I

Intervals (Part 1)

These triads consist of three alternate scale tones sounded simultaneously.

The interval between the lowest and middle note is a 3rd; the interval between the lowest and highest note is a 5th.

Rule: If the upper note of a 3rd is contained within the diatonic major scale of the lower note, it is major (M). If it is lowered, it is minor (m). If it is raised, it is augmented (+).

Fig. 14.

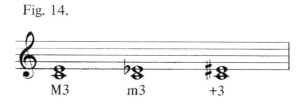

M3   m3   +3

Thus, in the Key of C:

I   Based on the scale of C, C-E is major (M)

II Based on the scale of D, D-F is minor (m)

III Based on the scale of E, E-G is minor (m)

IV Based on the scale of F, F-A is major (M)

V Based on the scale of G, G-B is major (M)

VI Based on the scale of A, A-C is minor (m)

VII Based on the scale of B, B-D is minor (m)

Fig. 15

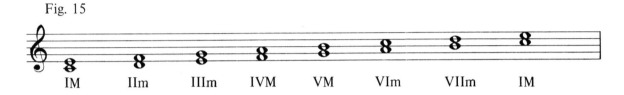

This is true in all keys

Rule: If the upper note of a 5th is contained within the diatonic major scale of the lower note, it is perfect (P). If it is lowered, it is diminished (o). If it is raised, it is augmented (+).

Fig. 16

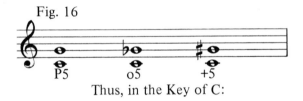

Thus, in the Key of C:

I   Based on the scale of C, C-G is perfect (P)

II Based on the scale of D, D-A is perfect (P)

III Based on the scale of E, E-B is perfect (P)

IV Based on the scale of F, F-C   is perfect (P)

V Based on the scale of G, G-D is perfect (P)

VI Based on the scale of A, A-E is perfect (P)

VII Based on the scale of B, B-F is diminished (o)

Fig. 17

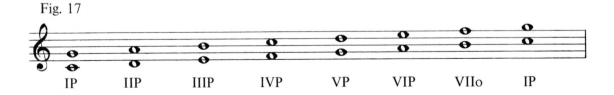

This is true in all keys

8

Combination		Position	Chord Quality
3rd	5th		
M	+	See note	augmented (+)
M	P	I - IV - V	major (M)
m	P	II - III - VI	minor (m)
m	o	VII	diminished (o)

Note: The augmented triad does not appear in the major diatonic system.(It does appear in the minor diatonic system.) It is included here because of its common usage in tunes.

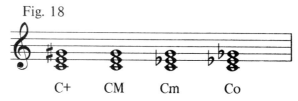

Fig. 18

C+   CM   Cm   Co

Rule: In any key, I, IV and V are major: II, III and VI are minor: VII is diminished. The augmented triad is added to the system.

Letters versus Numerals

Throughout this text the student will notice the interchangeable use of letters and numerals. Depending upon the specific problem under consideration, both are permissible. Illustrations, such as the Harmonic Vocabulary in which no key center is involved, obviously submit to lettered spelling; on the other hand, chord progressions or chord charts of tunes involving a key center demand the use of numerals in order to give the student a sense of key center unity which every experienced jazz musician uses as a natural process whether or not he or she is intellectually aware of the use of numerals. Numerals or figured bass (basso continuo) evolved during the Renaissance, and for some five centuries has been the classical vocabulary employed in music schools throughout the world. Ironically, improvisors in the classical tradition have historically employed numerals when performing in order to be free of the bondage of notation. Letters have never been employed (except for simple identification) in the classical field. The use of letters began in the early part of the of the present century; they were originally employed by the publishing industry to assist the average purchaser of sheet music in identifying ukulele or banjo chords. Since many of the early jazzmen were gifted but untrained musicians, they accepted the lettered chords as a readily available language in order to communicate with each other. However, when jazzmen perform, they "pre - hear" the next chord or phrase through a natural numerical estimate of where they are and where they are going. An added advantage involving numerals in progressions and chord charts should be apparent to the student. One set of numerals gives instantaneous twelve key facility since the numerals work for all keys. Otherwise, it would require twelve sets of letters to allow for transposition.

Chapter 2

The Seventh Chord System

Lesson: Play the scale - tone seventh chords of Fig. 1 through Fig. 13 in **both hands until** they can be played automatically from memory in any key.

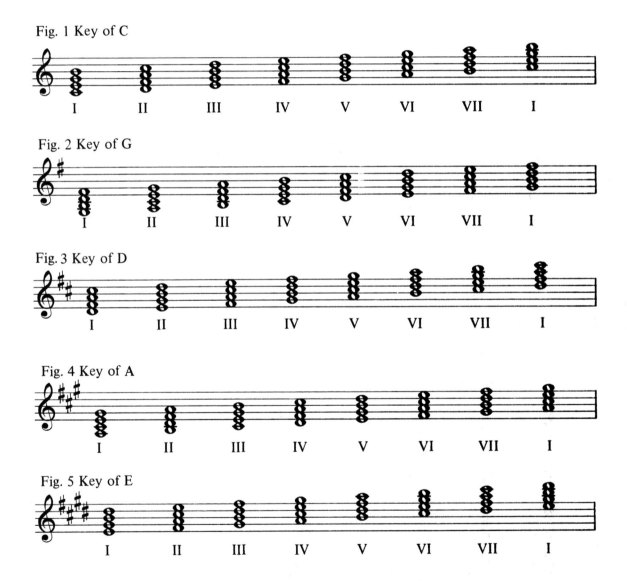

Fig. 1 Key of C

I   II   III   IV   V   VI   VII   I

Fig. 2 Key of G

I   II   III   IV   V   VI   VII   I

Fig. 3 Key of D

I   II   III   IV   V   VI   VII   I

Fig. 4 Key of A

I   II   III   IV   V   VI   VII   I

Fig. 5 Key of E

I   II   III   IV   V   VI   VII   I

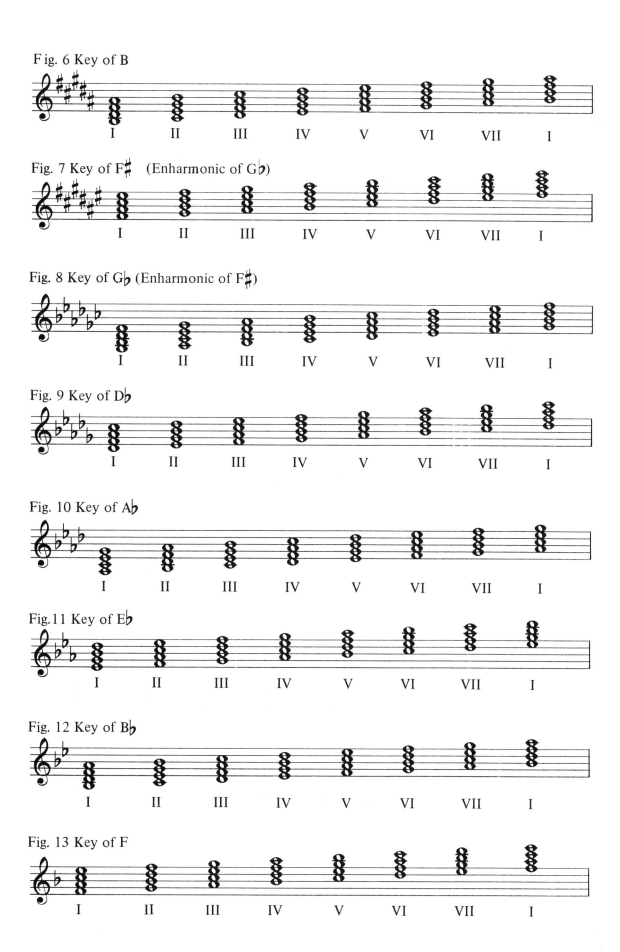

Fig. 6 Key of B

I II III IV V VI VII I

Fig. 7 Key of F♯ (Enharmonic of G♭)

I II III IV V VI VII I

Fig. 8 Key of G♭ (Enharmonic of F♯)

I II III IV V VI VII I

Fig. 9 Key of D♭

I II III IV V VI VII I

Fig. 10 Key of A♭

I II III IV V VI VII I

Fig.11 Key of E♭

I II III IV V VI VII I

Fig. 12 Key of B♭

I II III IV V VI VII I

Fig. 13 Key of F

I II III IV V VI VII I

Chapter 3

Intervals (Part 2)

On Pages 7 and 8 rules for thirds and fifths were presented. The following indicates the general rule for all intervals:

If the upper note of a 2nd, 3rd, 6th or 7th is contained within the diatonic major scale of the lower note, it is major (M). If it is lowered, it is minor (m). If it is raised, it is augmented (+).

Fig. 1

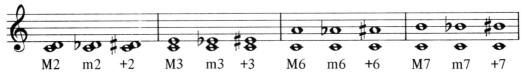

M2   m2   +2   M3   m3   +3   M6   m6   +6   M7   m7   +7

If the upper note of a 4th, 5th or 8th (octave) is contained within the diatonic major scale of the lower note, it is perfect (P). If it is lowered, it is diminished (o). If it is raised, it is augmented (+).

Fig. 2

P4   o4   +4   P5   o5   +5   P8   o8   +8

Fig. 3 Key of C

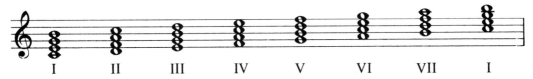

I   II   III   IV   V   VI   VII   I

   I   Based on the scale of C, C - E is major (M)
  II Based on the scale of D, D - F is minor (m)
III Based on the scale of E, E - G is minor (m)
IV Based on the scale of F, F - A is major (M)
  V Based on the scale of G, G - B is major (M)
VI Based on the scale of A, A - C is minor (m)
VII Based on the scale of B, B - D is minor(m)

   I   Based on the scale of C, C-G is perfect (P)
  II Based on the scale of D, D-A is perfect (P)
III Based on the scale of E, E-B is perfect (P)
IV Based on the scale of F, F-C is perfect (P)
  V Based on the scale of G, G-D is perfect (P)
VI Based on the scale of A, A-E is perfect (P)
VII Based on the scale of B, B-F is diminished (o)

I   Based on the scale of C, C-B is major (M)
II Based on the scale of D, D-C is minor (m)
III Based on the scale of E, E-D is minor (m)
IV Based on the scale of F, F-E is major (M)
V   Based on the scale of G, G-F is minor (m)
VI Based on the scale of A, A-G is minor (m)
VII Based on the scale of B, B-A is minor (m)

In all Keys:

Combination			Position	Chord Quality
3rd	5th	7th		
M	P	M	I - IV	major 7th
M	P	m	V	dominant 7th
m	P	m	II - III - VI	minor 7th
m	o	m	VII	half diminished 7th*

*Note: The term "half diminished" may be new to the student although it has wide usage in the classical nomenclature and, mainly through the efforts of the late Bill Evans, has begun to appear in contemporary jazz originals. The term is derived from the fact that the "full" diminished 7th chord (as we shall see) employs two diminished intervals (o5, o7), whereas the "half - diminished" chord employs only one diminished interval (o5).

Fig. 4

The Diminished Seventh Chord:

The diminished seventh chord does not appear in the major diatonic system. (It does appear in the minor diatonic system.) This chord contains a minor 3rd, a diminished 5th and a diminished 7th (lowered twice from the seventh scale position). (See Fig. 5)

Fig. 5

*Note: Although written as C - A, with the m 3rd and o 5th it remains a o7th.

The Sixty Chord System

Fig. 6. illustrates the Sixty Chord System used in jazz harmony. It consists of five different qualities which can be applied at any point on the keyboard.

There are twelve tones in the octave, each capable of supporting the five qualities; thus, the Sixty Chord System.

Transferring to sharps on m, ø, and o is for ease of "spelling" these chords.

Fig. 6

*Note: The use of the symbol x for the dominant chord is explained in the following chapter.

14

Chapter 4

The Seventh Chord Symbols

The Major Seventh Symbol:

With the exception of the recent use of a triangle symbol ($\triangle$), the traditional major symbol has always been either M7 or maj7. In this text the symbol M7 will be used.

The Dominant Seventh Symbol:

The traditional dominant symbols have always been 7 or 9 or 13 (C7, F9, etc.). The historical reason for this lay in the harmonic vocabulary of early jazz which employed the major triad, the minor triad, the diminished triad, the augmented triad and a fifth chord which demanded the use of the seventh, thus the 7 chord. Since all the seventh chords contain a seventh of some kind, it is apparent that the symbol 7 is improper. In this text the Juilliard symbol x7 will be used to indicate the dominant chord in any form (Cx7, E♭x7, B♭x9, etc.).

The Minor Seventh Symbol:

The traditional symbols for the minor seventh chord have been m7 or min.7. In this text the symbol m7 will be used.

The Half Diminished Symbol:

The half diminished symbol is only beginning to enter the public area. Traditionally it has been treated as minor 7♭5(m7-5) or its first inversion minor 6 (m6). The symbol for half diminished is ∅7 and will be employed in this text.

The Diminished Seventh Symbol:

The traditional symbols for diminished have been a zero (o) or dim. The text will employ o7 in referring to both intervals and chords.

The Minor Sixth Symbol:

The term minor sixth (m6) can mean different things at various times, e.g. sometimes Cm6 means a minor triad with an added sixth. (See Fig. 1)

Fig. 1

But, in some notation, the term Cm6 can really mean A∅7. Cm6(first inversion of A∅7) is the more familiar approximation of A∅7 or Am7♭5. In this text all root position ∅7 chords will be indicated as such; the minor sixth chord will appear as minor added sixth (m^{+6}) to avoid confusion with "6" as employed in inversions to be studied later. The same is true of major added sixth (M^{+6}).

Symbol Summary:

M^T = major triad
m^T = minor triad
o^T = diminished triad
+ = augmented triad
M7 = major seventh
x7 = dominant seventh
m7 = minor seventh
∅7 = half diminished seventh
o7 = diminished seventh
M^{+6} = major added 6th
m^{+6} = minor added 6th

Fig. 2 Key of C

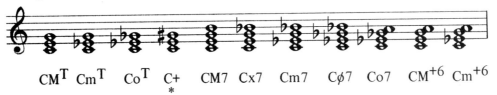

CM^T Cm^T Co^T C+ CM7 Cx7 Cm7 C∅7 Co7 CM^{+6} Cm^{+6}
                    *

*Note: The augmented triad is not indicated by "T" since the augmented chord does not appear in the seventh chord system.

See the complete Harmonic Vocabulary in Chapter 8 for further illustration of the total system.

Chapter 5

Altered Triads

The triads appearing in Chapter I and the seventh chords in Chapter 2 are shown
in their primary functions; in other words, as the scale naturally forms them.
If our use of harmony was limited to these primary functions we would be unable
to perform even the simplest jazz material.
Fortunately, the diatonic system readily lends itself to alteration. These alterations
sub - divide into secondary functions and tertiary functions.

Secondary Functions:
Rule: A secondary function involves the raising or
lowering of the 3rd and/or 5th of a triad; or the 3rd, 5th and/or 7th of a seventh chord
to form a new chord or quality on any tone of the scale. (See Fig. 1.)

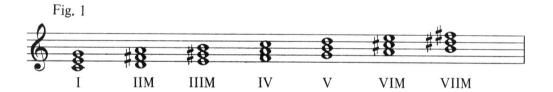

Fig. 1

I   IIM   IIIM   IV   V   VIM   VIIM

In Fig. 1 the triads I - IV - V are naturally major;
II - III - VI are minor which required raising the third in each case;
VII is diminished which required raising both third and fifth in order to
form major.

The following alteration table describes the intervals to be altered in order to form various triad qualities. (See Fig. 2)

Fig. 2

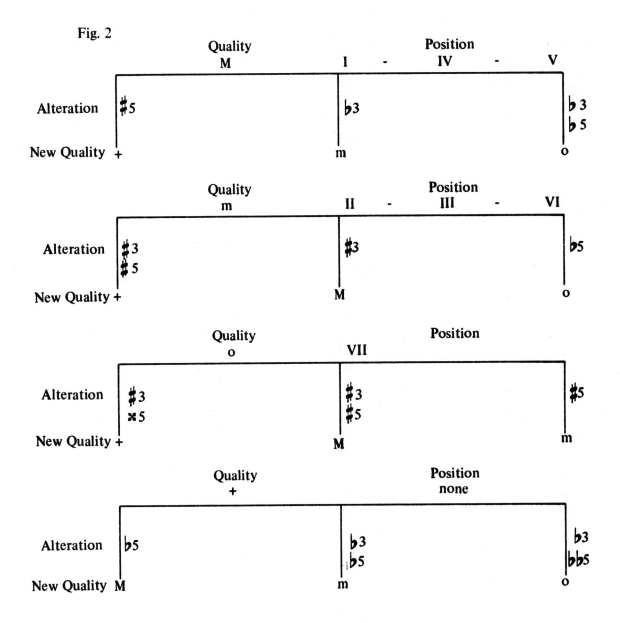

Lesson:

Complete the following triad qualities. Check your result against the Harmonic Vocabulary in Chapter 8.

Fig. 3

C+   Gm   Do   AM   E♭+   Bm   F♯m   G♭o   D♭M   A♭+   E♭m   B♭o   F+   Co

Tertiary Functions:

Rule:

A tertiary function involves raising or lowering an altered or unaltered chord chromatically out of the key. (See Fig. 4)

Fig. 4 Key of C

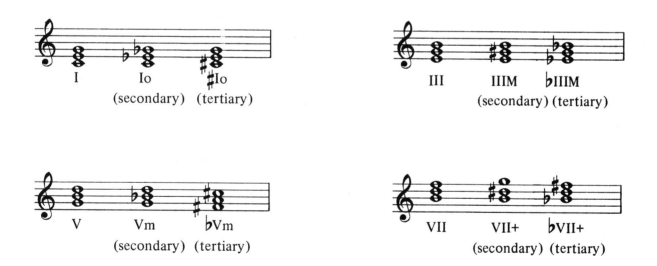

Rule:

In the chromatic harmonic system of jazz any chord can be built on any tone in the chromatic scale by altering, lowering or raising any chord in the diatonic system.

Chapter 6

Altered Seventh Chords

Triad harmony is used extensively in rock, country music and folk music as it was in Dixieland jazz from 1900 to 1920. In this period the only 7th chord employed was the dominant 7th but, gradually, through the twenties and into the early thirties, the seventh chord system began to replace the triad system until by 1934, with the development of the Goodman and Ellington bands, the seventh chord system with its extensive use of 9ths,11ths and 13ths became the lasting language of jazz.

Secondary and Tertiary Functions:

As indicated in Chapter 5, the secondary and tertiary functions are formed by altering the 3rd, 5th and/or 7th or by lowering or raising the chord chromatically. See Fig. 1.

Fig. 1 Key of C

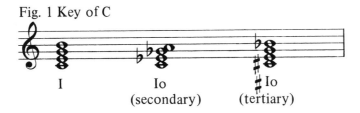

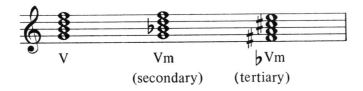

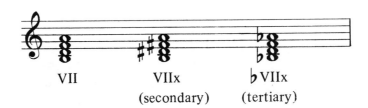

Lesson:

Fig. 5 is an original tune employing the triad chromatic harmonic system.

The use of the symbol T will not be necessary since the piece consists entirely of triads.

Practice Fig. 5 until it can be played without hesitation.

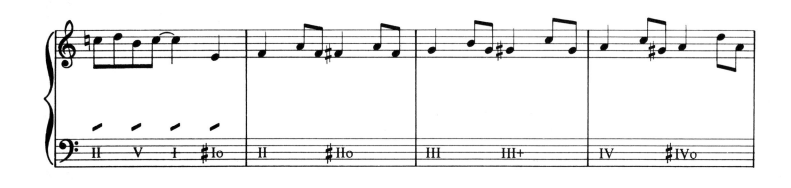

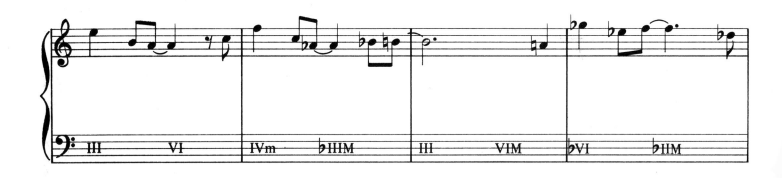

The following alteration table describes the intervals to be altered in order to form various seventh chord qualities.

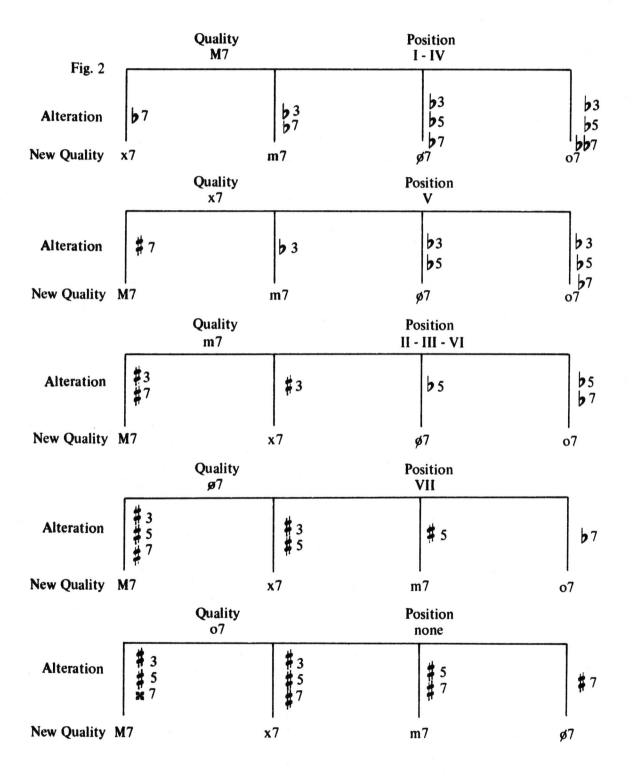

Fig. 2

Lesson:

    Fig. 3 is an original tune employing the seventh chord chromatic harmonic system.

    The use of the Arabic numeral 7 will not be necessary since there are no triads in the piece.

    Practice Fig. 3 until it can be played without hesitation.

Fig. 3 Key of C

* Note: The x♭5 chords in measures 3, 4, 11, 12, 27 and 28 should be played with the anticipated (tied) figures;
    also the m chords in measures 5, 6, 13, 14, 29 and 30.

Chapter 7

Inversions

Inversions (Triads)

An inversion results from re-arranging the tones of a chord in such a way that the root of the chord is no longer in the bass. (See Fig. 1)

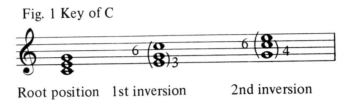

Fig. 1 Key of C

Root position   1st inversion   2nd inversion

The traditional symbols for triad inversions are formed by counting the number of scale tones from the bass note to each of the remaining tones in the chord. Thus, in Fig. 1 the distance from E to C in the first inversion is a 6th; the distance from E to G is a 3rd. Thus, the symbol for first inversion is $\frac{6}{3}$ or, more usually, 6. In the second inversion the distance from G to E is a 6th; the distance from G to C is a 4th. Thus the symbol for second inversion is $\frac{6}{4}$ and that is never modified. Fig. 2 illustrates the triads of C with their inversions.

Fig. 2 Scale-tone triads of C and their inversions.

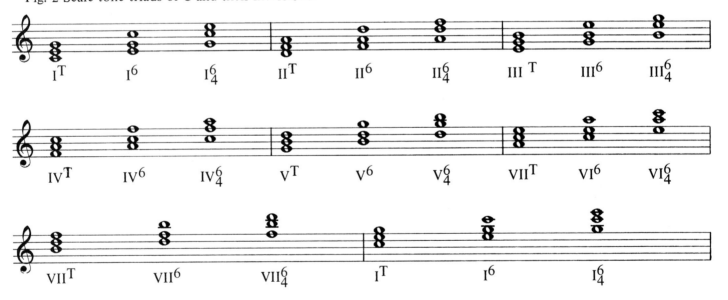

Lesson: Practice the scale-tone triads and their inversions in twelve keys - both hands.

Inversions (Seventh Chords)

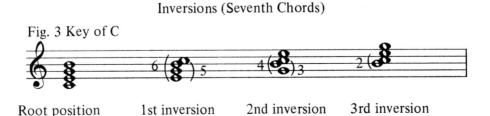

Fig. 3 Key of C

Root position   1st inversion   2nd inversion   3rd inversion

Each inversion of a seventh chord contains an interval of a second
(B - C in Fig.3). The symbol for the inversion is formed by counting the
scale - tones from the bass note to each of the notes of the second.
Thus, in Fig. 3, in the first inversion, E to C is a 6th; E to B is a 5th.
Thus, the symbol is $\frac{6}{5}$. In the second inversion, G to C is a 4th; G to B is a 3rd.
Thus, the symbol is $\frac{4}{3}$. In the third inversion B to C is a 2nd.
Thus, the symbol is 2.
Fig. 4 illustrates the seventh chords of C with their inversions.

Fig. 4 Scale - tone seventh chords of C with their inversions.

Lesson: Practice the scale-tone seventh chords and their inversions in twelve keys - both hands.

Note: The student will note in Chapter 8 that the diminished seventh chord cannot be inverted since the tones are evenly spaced by minor thirds and no tone is adjacent to another. Of all the chords we have studied only the diminished seventh never loses its original intervals.

Chapter 8

The Harmonic Vocabulary

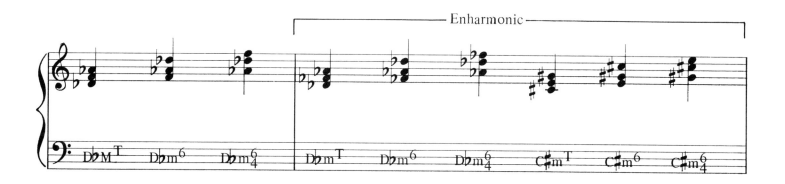

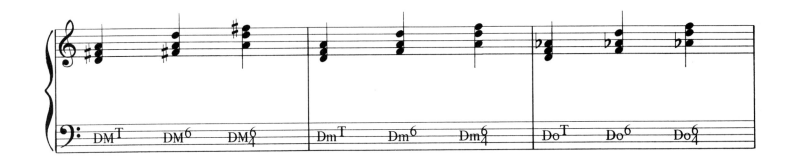

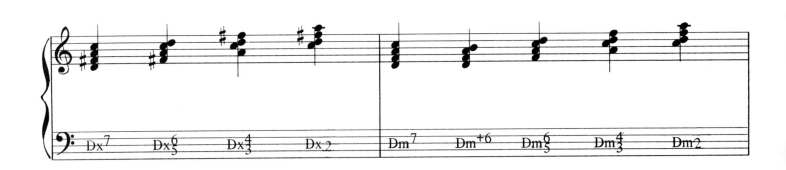

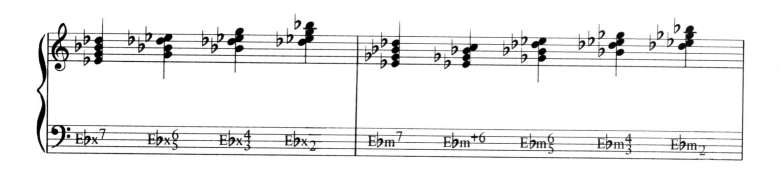

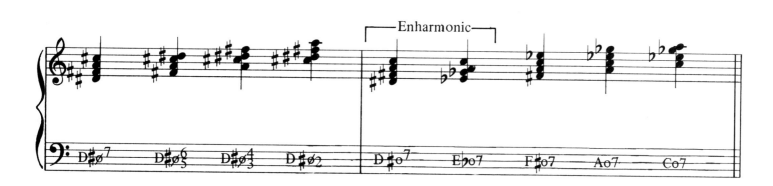

31

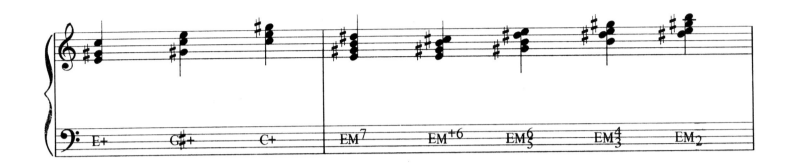

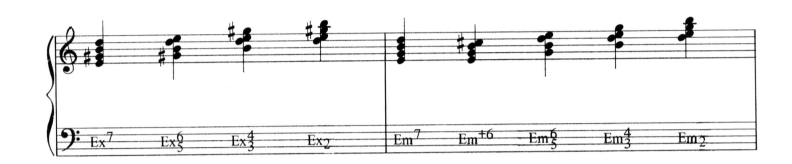

Enharmonic

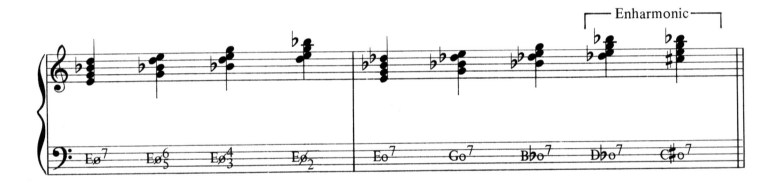

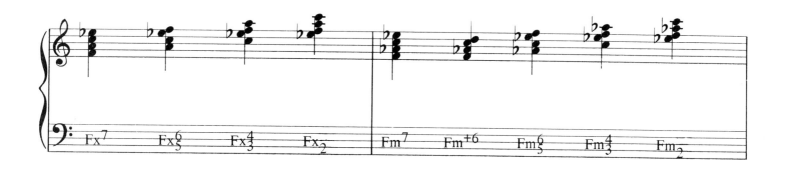

$\text{Fx}^7 \qquad \text{Fx}^6_5 \qquad \text{Fx}^4_3 \qquad \text{Fx}_2 \qquad \text{Fm}^7 \qquad \text{Fm}^{+6} \qquad \text{Fm}^6_5 \qquad \text{Fm}^4_3 \qquad \text{Fm}_2$

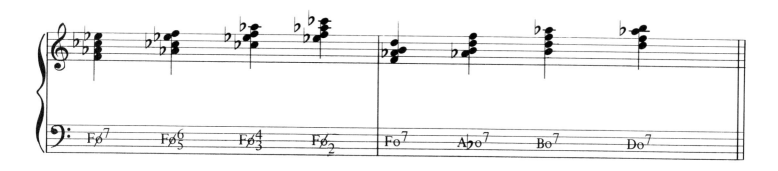

$\text{F}ø^7 \qquad \text{F}ø^6_5 \qquad \text{F}ø^4_3 \qquad \text{F}ø_2 \qquad \text{Fo}^7 \qquad \text{A}♭\text{o}^7 \qquad \text{Bo}^7 \qquad \text{Do}^7$

Enharmonic

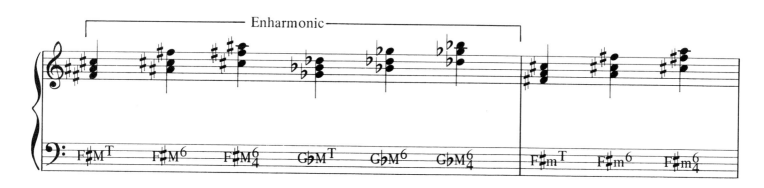

$\text{F}\sharp\text{M}^T \qquad \text{F}\sharp\text{M}^6 \qquad \text{F}\sharp\text{M}^6_4 \qquad \text{G}♭\text{M}^T \qquad \text{G}♭\text{M}^6 \qquad \text{G}♭\text{M}^6_4 \qquad \text{F}\sharp\text{m}^T \qquad \text{F}\sharp\text{m}^6 \qquad \text{F}\sharp\text{m}^6_4$

$\text{F}\sharp\text{o}^T \qquad \text{F}\sharp\text{o}^6 \qquad \text{F}\sharp\text{o}^6_4 \qquad \text{F}\sharp+ \qquad \text{A}\sharp+ \qquad \text{D}+$

Enharmonic

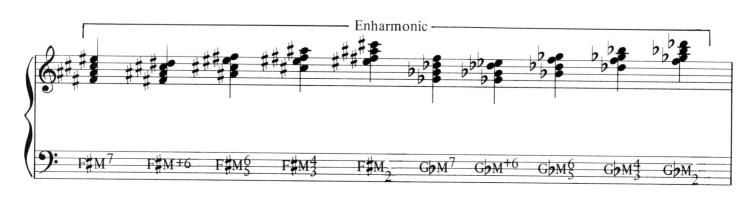

$\text{F}\sharp\text{M}^7 \quad \text{F}\sharp\text{M}^{+6} \quad \text{F}\sharp\text{M}^6_5 \quad \text{F}\sharp\text{M}^4_3 \quad \text{F}\sharp\text{M}_2 \quad \text{G}♭\text{M}^7 \quad \text{G}♭\text{M}^{+6} \quad \text{G}♭\text{M}^6_5 \quad \text{G}♭\text{M}^4_3 \quad \text{G}♭\text{M}_2$

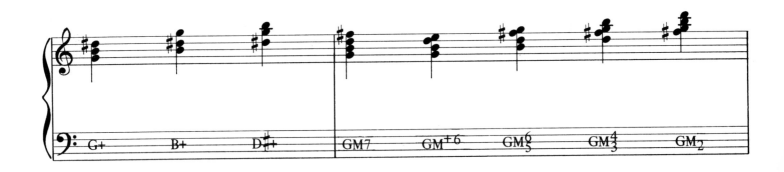

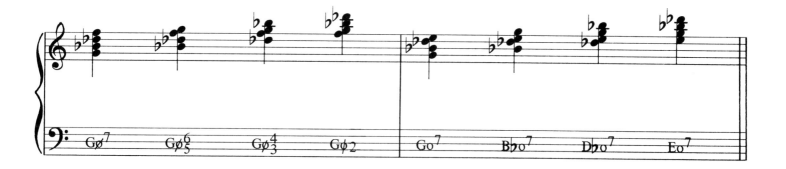

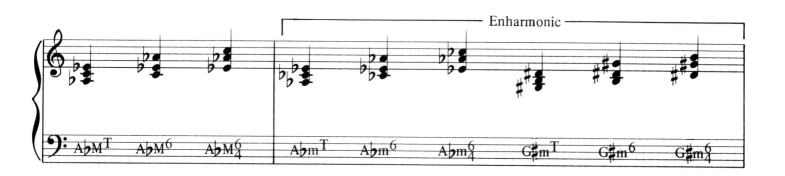

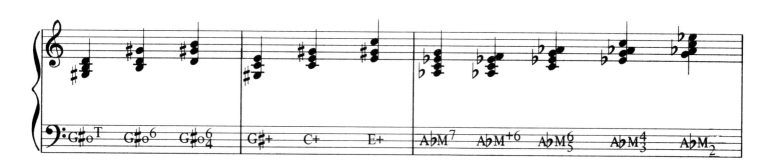

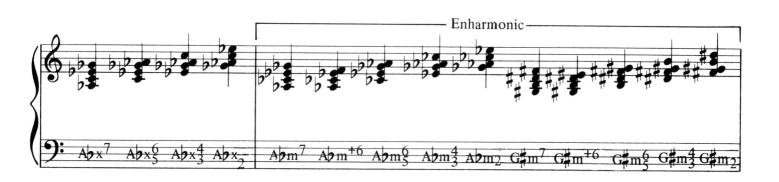

— Enharmonic —

— Enharmonic —

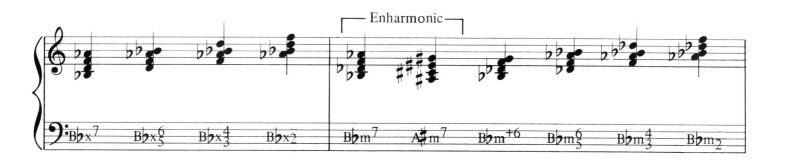

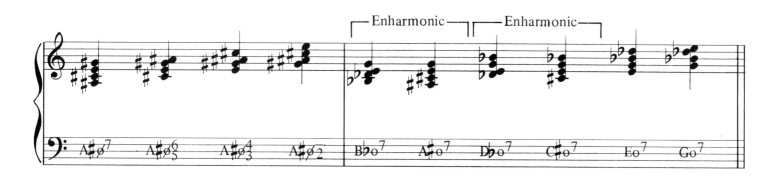

Note: From this point onward the use of the Arabic numeral 7 will no longer be necessary. All chords are seventh chords unless indicated otherwise.

Chapter 9

Jazz Rhythm

Improvisation in both Western and Eastern music has flourished for centuries; only since 1900 has improvisation in Western classical music declined, coinciding with the rise of jazz improvisation - a unique fusion of African rhythm and European harmony.

These unique qualities of jazz improvisation lie in the following:

1. The African device of accenting unstressed portions of the bar.

2. The specific rhythmic assignments usually employed as follows:

> Rhythmic unit = Quarter note (♩)
> Harmonic unit = Quarter note (♩)
>   Half note (♩)
>   Whole note (o)

> Melodic unit   = Eighth notes (♪ ♪)
>   Eighth note triplets (♪ ♪ ♪)
>   Sixteenth notes   (♬ ♬)
>   Sixteenth note triplets (♬♬ ♬♬)

The following historical treatments of the twelve - bar blues will illustrate how each style has employed these three units.

Chapter 10

Ragtime/Stride Piano
1900 - 1920

Rhythmic unit = ♩ (swing bass octaves)
Harmonic unit = ♩ and ♩ (combination of ♩ swing bass and ♩ "walk" bars)
Melodic unit   = ♩ and ♫

The student is encouraged to seek out recordings of the following practitioners of this style:

> "Jelly Roll" Morton
> James P. Johnson
> Willie "The Lion" Smith
> "Fats" Waller (early)
> Tom Turpin
> James Scott
> Scott Joplin

Fig. I. Key of B♭

* P.N. = passing note

Chorus 2

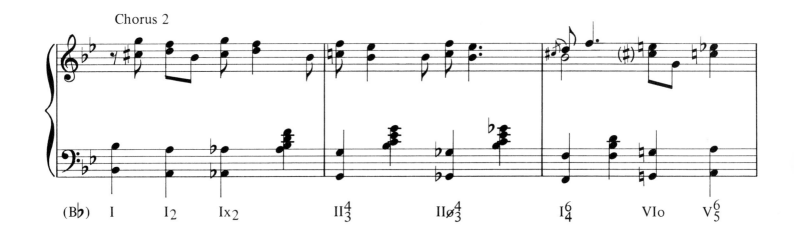

$(B\flat)$ I I_2 Ix_2 II_3^4 $II\emptyset_3^4$ I_4^6 VIo V_5^6

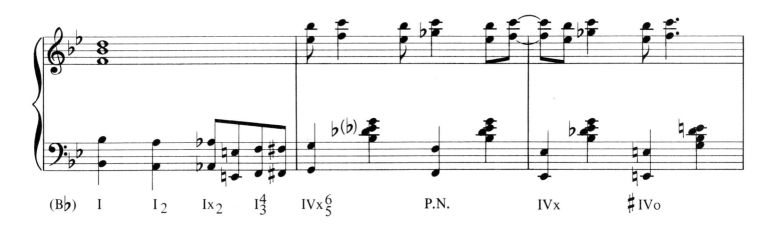

$(B\flat)$ I I_2 Ix_2 I_3^4 IVx_5^6 P.N.   IVx $\sharp$IVo

$(B\flat)$ I_4^6 V_2 VI_3^4 $\flat$IIIo   II   P.N.   IV $\sharp$IVo

$(B\flat)$ V   VI $\sharp$VIo V_5^6 I I^6 IV $\sharp$IVo   V   I

Chapter 11

Swing Piano
1920 - 1940

Rhythmic unit = ♩ (swing bass tenths)

Harmonic unit = ♩ and ♩ (combination of ♩ swing bass and ♩ "walk" bars

Melodic unit = ♩, ♫ , ♫♪ and ♬

The student is encouraged to seek out recordings of the following stylists of this period:

> "Fats" Waller (middle, late periods)
> Earl Hines
> Art Tatum
> Teddy Wilson

Tenths

Tenths break down into three spans:

Span 1	Span 2	Span 3
C - E♭	C - E	D♭ - F
C♯ - E	D - F	D - F♯
F - A♭	D♯ - F♯	E♭ - G
F♯ - A	E - G	E - G♯
G - B♭	F - A	F♯ - A♯
G♯ - B	G - B	A♭ - C
	A - C	A - C♯
	B♭ - D♭	B♭ - D
	B - D	B - D♯

Spans 1 and 2 are within the normal hand span of the average pianist; span 3 is not and will be avoided in this text.

Fig. 1 illustrates swing piano: the first chorus is in the general style of Teddy Wilson, the second is more reminiscent of Art Tatum.

Fig. 1. Key of C

Chorus 2

(C) Ix   Io   IIø2   I   V/I

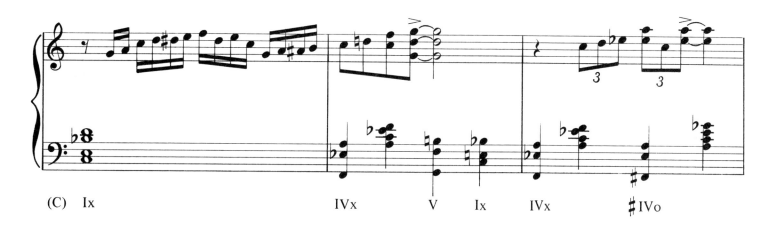

(C) Ix   IVx   V   Ix   IVx   ♯IVo

(C) Ix$_3^4$ ♭VIIx$_3^4$ VIx$_3^4$ V$_3^4$ ♯Io   II   VIx$_3^4$ II^6 ♯IVo

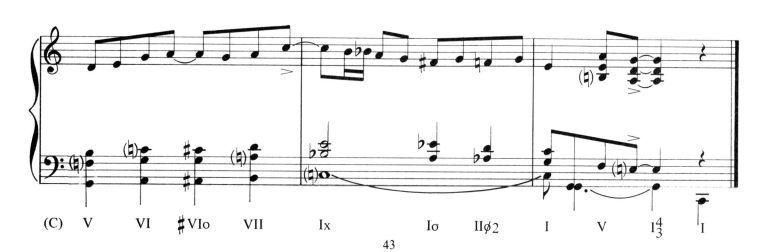

(C) V   VI   ♯VIo   VII   Ix   Io   IIø2   I   V   I$_3^4$ I

Chapter 12

Bop Piano
1940 - 1955

Rhythmic unit = ♩ (foot beat)

Harmonic unit = ♩ and 𝅝 (left hand "shells")

Melodic unit = [notation] , [notation] and [notation]

The important pianists of the early revolutionary period of bop were:

> Earl "Bud" Powell
> Thelonious Monk

Powell in particular forged a style which would accommodate the new demands of bop:

> avoidance of swing bass
> left hand shells (chord fragments)
> right hand "horn line"

In the later period of bop the major influential pianists were:

> Horace Silver
> Hampton Hawes

Shells

The use of shells are illustrated in Fig 1; they usually employ the root and the 7th or the root and the 3rd.

The fingerings usually employed are as follows:

> Root and 7th = 5th finger and thumb.
> Root and 3rd = 2nd finger and thumb.

Fig. 1 Key of F

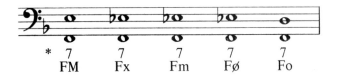

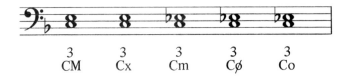

*Note: The numerals above the chord names indicate the interval point of the left hand shell.

Since a shell can only imply the quality of a chord, the following table will be helpful in determining the function of each shell in Fig. 1.

Shell		Implied Quality
M 7th	=	M 7 chord
m 7th	=	$\begin{cases} \text{x 7 chord} \\ \text{m 7 chord} \\ \text{ø 7 chord} \end{cases}$
o 7th	=	o 7 chord
M 3rd	=	$\begin{cases} \text{M 7 chord} \\ \text{x 7 chord} \end{cases}$
m 3rd	=	$\begin{cases} \text{m 7 chord} \\ \text{ø 7 chord} \\ \text{o 7 chord} \end{cases}$

45

Fig. 2 illustrates a drill which should be practiced around the circle of fifths from the twelve major thirds. The fingering is always 2 - 1 for 3rds and 5 - 1 for 7ths.

Fig. 2
Key of C   Left Hand Drill

Key of D♭

Key of D

Key of E♭

Key of E

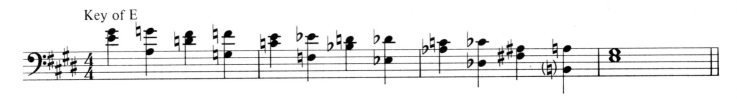

Fig. 3 is a treatment of the twelve - bar blues in the characteristic style of bop piano.

Fig. 3   Key of B♭

Lively

Introduction

(B♭)   III⁷   ♭III⁷   II⁷

Chorus 1

(B♭)   II⁷   ♭IIx⁷   I⁷   IV³   VII⁷   IIIx³   VI⁷   IIx³

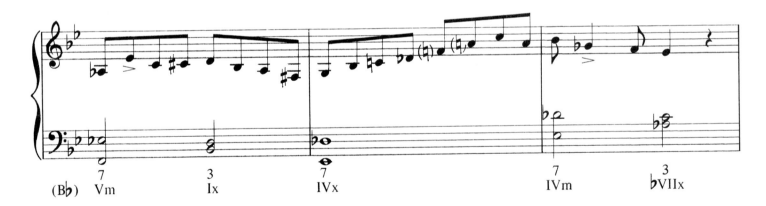

(B♭)   Vm⁷   Ix³   IVx⁷   IVm⁷   ♭VIIx³

(B♭)   III⁷   VIx³   ♭III⁷   ♭VIx³   II⁷

* All inversion shells employ the outside voices of the particular inversion forming a point of six.

Chapter 13

Early Contemporary Jazz Piano
1955 - 1965

Rhythmic unit = ♩ (foot beat)

Harmonic unit = ♩ and 𝅝 (left hand voicings)

Melodic unit = ♫ , ♫♪ , ♬♬ and ♬♬♬♬

In the middle fifties stylistic changes in jazz piano began to be heard, particularly in the Miles Davis rhythm sections of the period. The important pianists in this early movement were:

"Red" Garland

Wynton Kelly

The basic problem of early contemporary jazz piano was to escape from the severe three voice style of bop piano into a more harmonic approach. This was achieved through the use of left hand voicings which will be thoroughly studied further on in this book.

Fig. 1 illustrates this style applied to the twelve - bar blues.

Fig. 1 Key of B♭

Medium

Chorus 1

(B♭)　　Ix　　　　　　　　　　♭IIx　　　　　　　　Ix

(B♭)　♭IIx　　　　　Ix　　　　　IVx　　　　♯IVx　　　　IVx

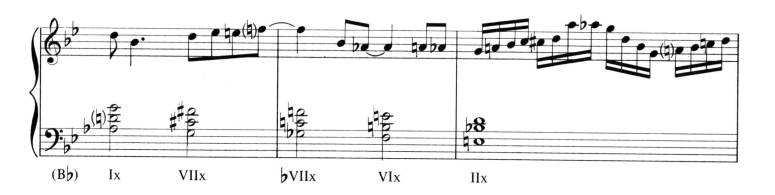

(B♭)　　Ix　　　VIIx　　　　♭VIIx　　　VIx　　　IIx

(B♭)♭IIx　　　　　　　　　Ix　　　　♭IIIx　　　　IIx　　　♭IIx

Chorus 2

(B♭)   Ix   IVx   Ix   ♭IIx

(B♭)   Ix   IVx

(B♭)   IVx   Ix   VIIx   ♭VIIx   VIx

(B♭)   IIx   ♭IIx

(B♭)   Ix   ♭IIx   Ix

Chapter 14

Contemporary Jazz Piano
1965 - Present

Rhythmic unit = ♩ (foot beat)

Harmonic unit = ♩ and 𝅝 (left hand voicings / modal fourth fragments)

Melodic unit = 𝅘𝅥𝅮 𝅘𝅥𝅮, 𝅘𝅥𝅮 𝅘𝅥𝅮 𝅘𝅥𝅮, 𝅘𝅥𝅯𝅘𝅥𝅯𝅘𝅥𝅯𝅘𝅥𝅯 and 𝅘𝅥𝅯𝅘𝅥𝅯𝅘𝅥𝅯𝅘𝅥𝅯𝅘𝅥𝅯𝅘𝅥𝅯𝅘𝅥𝅯𝅘𝅥𝅯

Many of the further developments of contemporary jazz piano continued to occur in the Miles Davis rhythm sections with the appearance of Bill Evans, Herbie Hancock and Chick Corea. An exception was McCoy Tyner who achieved his innovations with John Coltrane.

The student should study carefully the recordings of:

> Bill Evans
> Herbie Hancock
> Chick Corea
> McCoy Tyner

Fig. 1 illustrates some of the basic devices employed by contemporary pianists as they would appear in the twelve - bar blues.

Fig. 1   Key of C

Brightly

Chorus 1

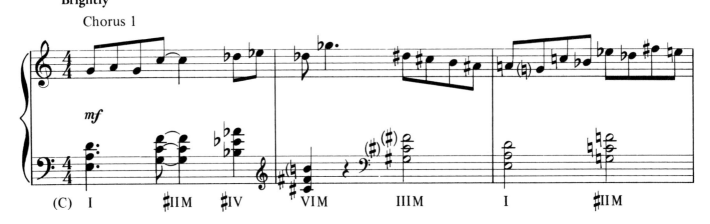

(C)   I   ♯IIM   ♯IV   VIM   IIIM   I   ♯IIM

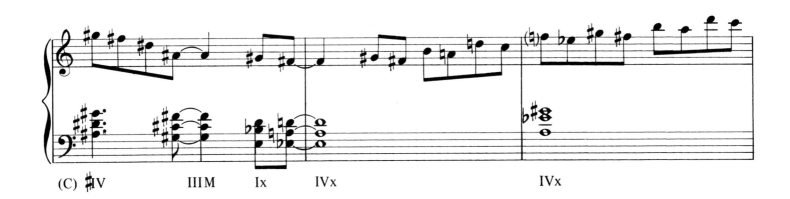

(C)   ♯IV   IIIM   Ix   IVx   IVx

(C)   Ix   VIIx   ♭VIIx   VIx   IIx

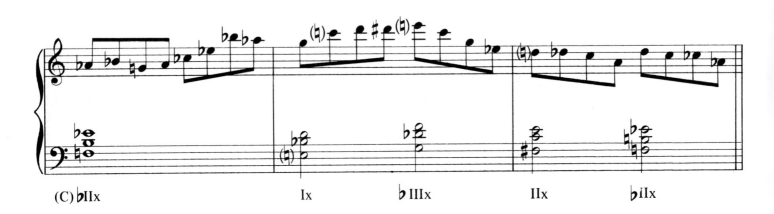

(C) ♭IIx   Ix   ♭IIIx   IIx   ♭iIx

54

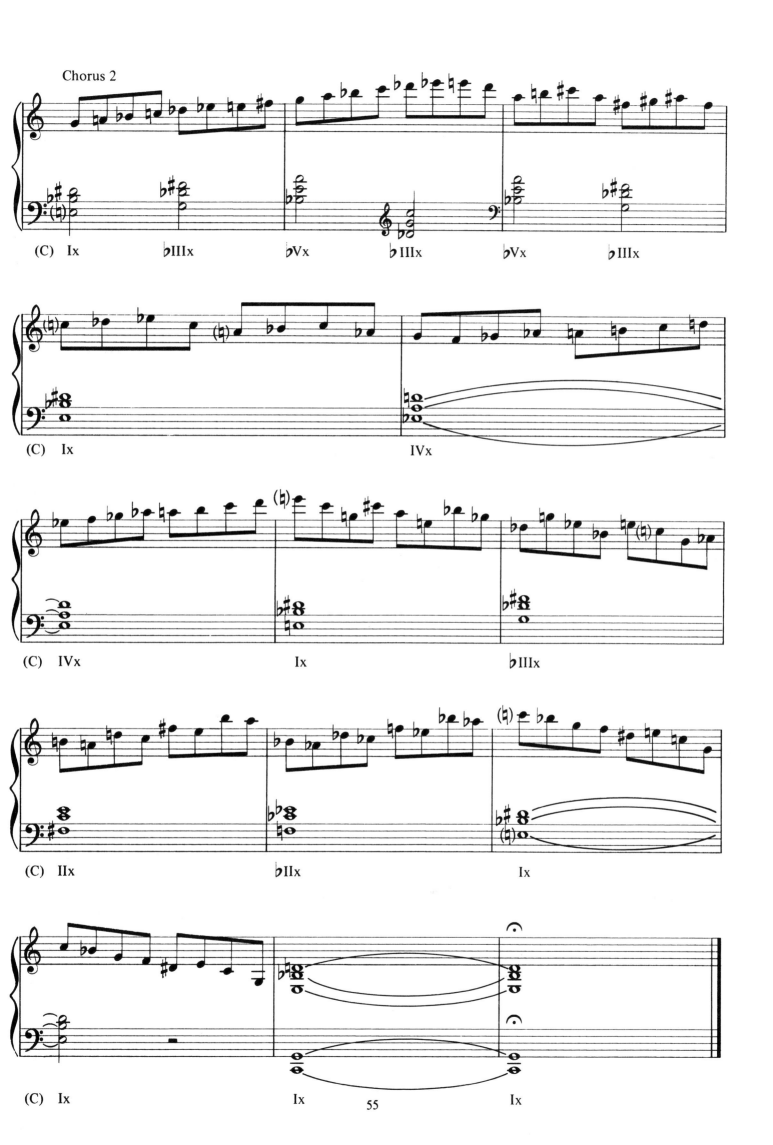

Chorus 2

(C) Ix   ♭IIIx   ♭Vx   ♭IIIx   ♭Vx   ♭IIIx

(C) Ix   IVx

(C) IVx   Ix   ♭IIIx

(C) IIx   ♭IIx   Ix

(C) Ix   Ix   Ix

55

The student may notice the absence of several important pianists in the preceding summary, in particular Oscar Peterson and George Shearing. These omissions demand an explanation.

Oscar Peterson has established a level of virtuosity in jazz piano reminiscent of the great Art Tatum. Peterson's influences, however, are more modern - namely Bud Powell, Charlie Parker, George Shearing and Nat Cole. There are no major innovations in Peterson's playing as regards devices; his contribution lies in his brilliant consolidation of elements of the art from the time he first appeared on the jazz horizon in 1950.

George Shearing is a different matter. He is basically a Powell influenced pianist but is credited with developing and popularizing the block chord system previously associated with pianist Milt Buckner of the Lionel Hampton Band. This block chord system has become part of the jazz vernacular and is employed by many contemporary pianists in varying ways.

Two other pianists who left no heritage of devices employed by professional musicians but who brought jazz piano to the forefront of the American music public are Dave Brubeck and Erroll Garner. Both of these men were able to open new markets which had previously been largely inaccessible to jazz musicians. Brubeck, in colleges throughout the world; and Garner, through television and extensive recordings, brought a valuable exposure to jazz.

Chapter 15

The Improvised Line

Jazz improvisation involves abandoning the melody and creating an improvised line based on the resources of the chords.

These resources consist of the following:

       1. Arpeggios (broken chords)

       2. Modes

       3. Non - modal tones (blue notes)

Arpeggios

Fig. 1   Key of C

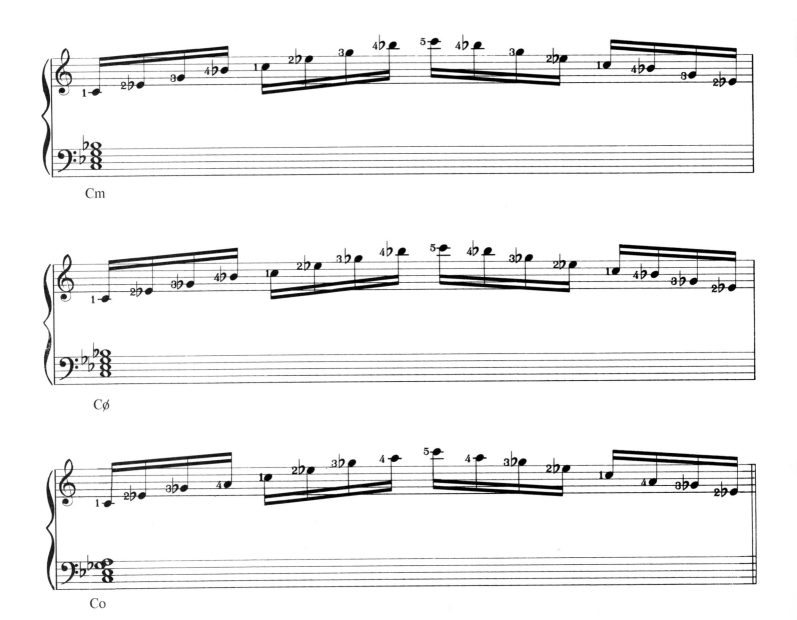

Cm

Cø

Co

The following table illustrates the right hand arpeggio fingerings for the Sixty chords. (See Chapter Three)
Inversion fingerings are generally derived from root position fingerings.
Some fingerings employ only one fingering combination for all five qualities (M, x, m, ø, o); others
require various fingerings as the intervals change.
The traditional rule concerning all fingering has been to avoid the thumb and, to some extent,
the fifth finger on black notes in order not to disturb the classic piano hand position.

C	M, x, m, φ, o	123412345 - reverse
D	M, x, m, φ, o	123412345 - reverse
E	M, x, m, φ, o	123412345 - reverse
F	M, x, m, φ, o	123412345 - reverse
G	M, x, m, φ, o	123412345 - reverse
A	M, x, m, φ, o	123412345 - reverse
B	M, x, m, φ, o	123412345 - reverse
D♭	M, x, m, φ, o	212341234 - reverse
A♭	M, x, m, φ, o	212341234 - reverse
B♭ (A♯)	M, x,	212341234 - reverse
B♭ (A♯)	m. φ, o	231234123 - reverse
G♭ (F♯)	M, x,	234123412 - reverse
G♭ (F♯)	m, φ, o	212341234 - reverse
E♭	M, x,	212341234 - reverse
E♭	m,	123412345 - reverse
E♭ (D♯)	φ, o	231234123 - reverse

Fig. 2 is an arpeggiated improvised line on "Here's That Rainy Day". Note the key changes.

The improvised line employs the ♪♪, ♪♪♪ (3) and ♪♪♪♪ melodic units.

The left hand shells create a basic bop treatment in order to lend a sense of style to the study.

The student is advised to seriously study the arpeggio table appearing above for automatic facility.

Here's That Rainy Day

words and music by
Johnny Burke and James Van Heusen

61

Chapter 16

Modes

A mode is a displaced scale starting on any tone in the row.

Thus, the scale of C can be played from:

I   C to C - Ionian Mode
II   D to D - Dorian Mode
III E to E - Phrygian Mode
IV F to F - Lydian Mode
V   G to G - Mixolydian Mode
VI A to A - Aeolian Mode
VII B to B - Locrian Mode

The terms appearing in the above table are the traditional Greek names applied to the modal displacements.

The basic problem here is to connect the eighty - four modes, (twelve scales, seven displacements) to the Sixty chord system in order to employ the most important device in contemporary jazz improvisation.

The Eighty-four Modes

(All fingerings follow the original Ionian fingering system)

Key of C

Ionian of C

I

Dorian of C

II

Phrygian of C

III

Lydian of C

IV

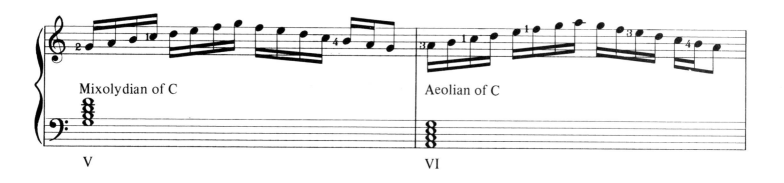

Mixolydian of C

V

Aeolian of C

VI

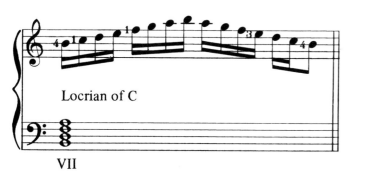

Locrian of C

VII

Key of D♭

Ionian of D♭

I

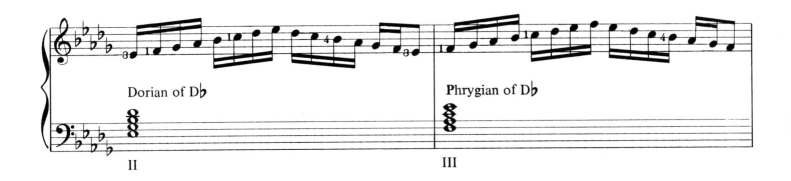

Dorian of D♭

II

Phrygian of D♭

III

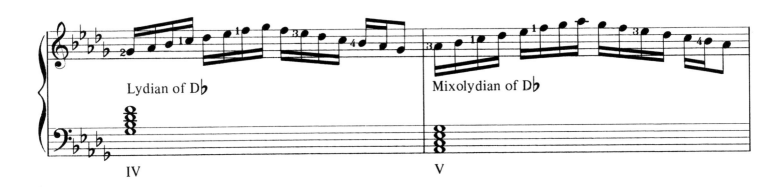

Lydian of D♭

IV

Mixolydian of D♭

V

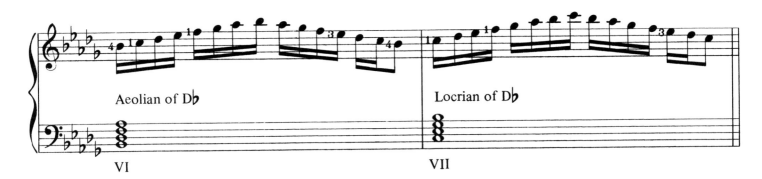

Aeolian of D♭

VI

Locrian of D♭

VII

Key of D

Ionian of D

I

Dorian of D

II

Phrygian of D

III

Lydian of D

IV

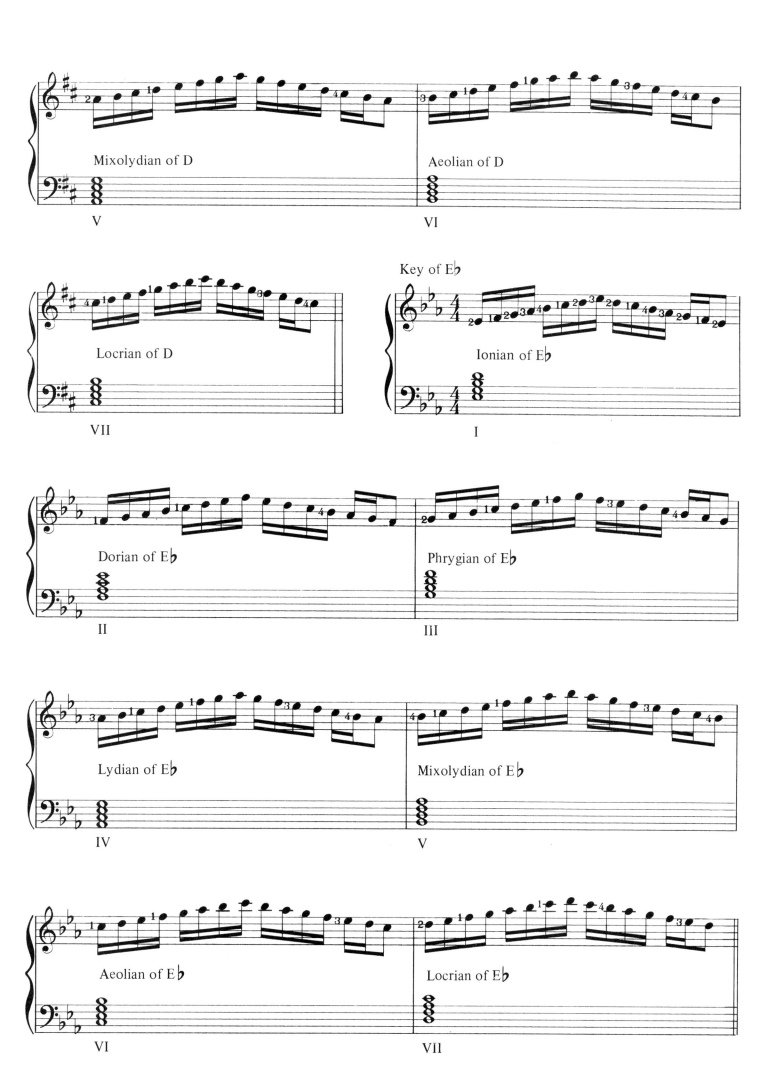

Mixolydian of D

V

Aeolian of D

VI

Locrian of D

VII

Key of E♭

Ionian of E♭

I

Dorian of E♭

II

Phrygian of E♭

III

Lydian of E♭

IV

Mixolydian of E♭

V

Aeolian of E♭

VI

Locrian of E♭

VII

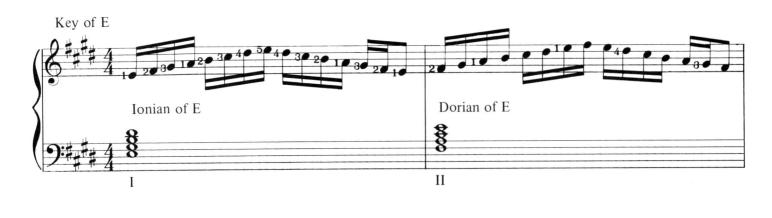

Key of E

Ionian of E

I

Dorian of E

II

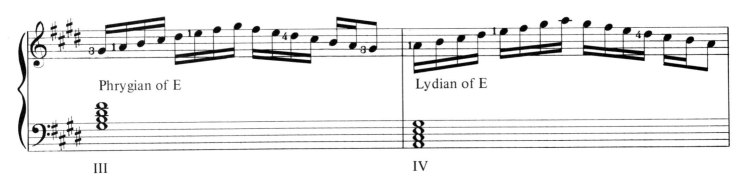

Phrygian of E

III

Lydian of E

IV

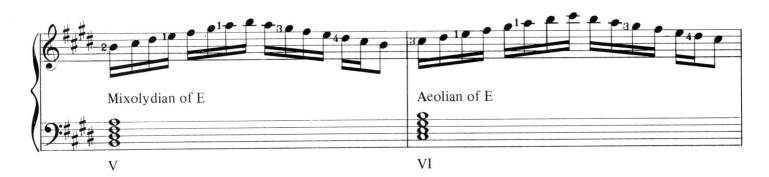

Mixolydian of E

V

Aeolian of E

VI

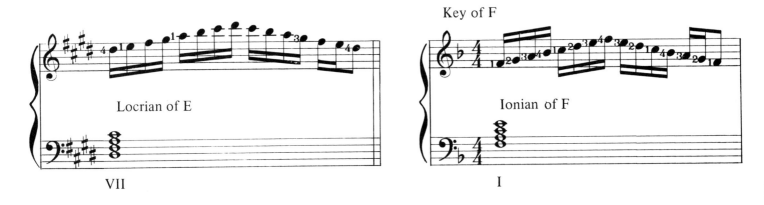

Locrian of E

VII

Key of F

Ionian of F

I

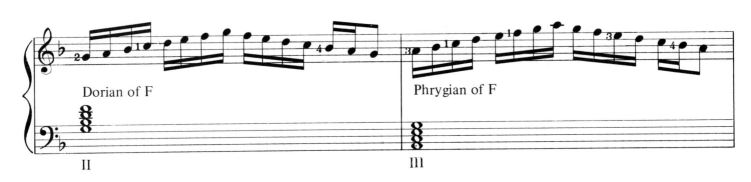

Dorian of F

II

Phrygian of F

III

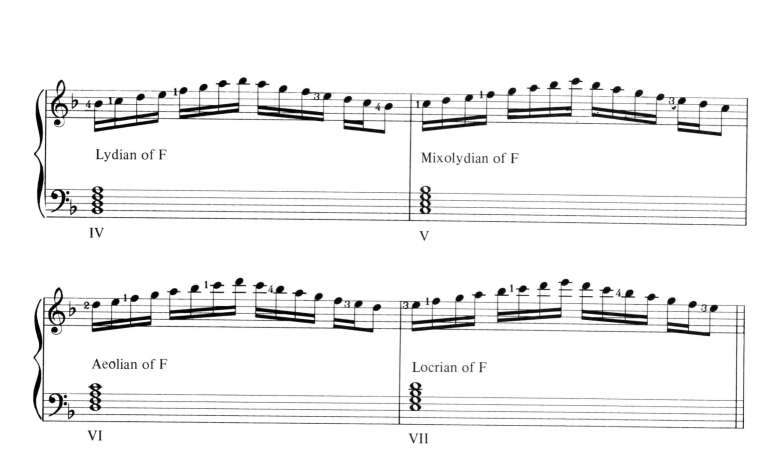

Lydian of F

IV

Mixolydian of F

V

Aeolian of F

VI

Locrian of F

VII

Key of F♯ (Enharmonic of G♭)

Ionian of F♯

I

Dorian of F♯

II

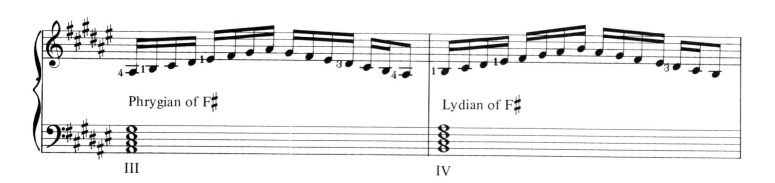

Phrygian of F♯

III

Lydian of F♯

IV

Mixolydian of F♯

V

Aeolian of F♯

VI

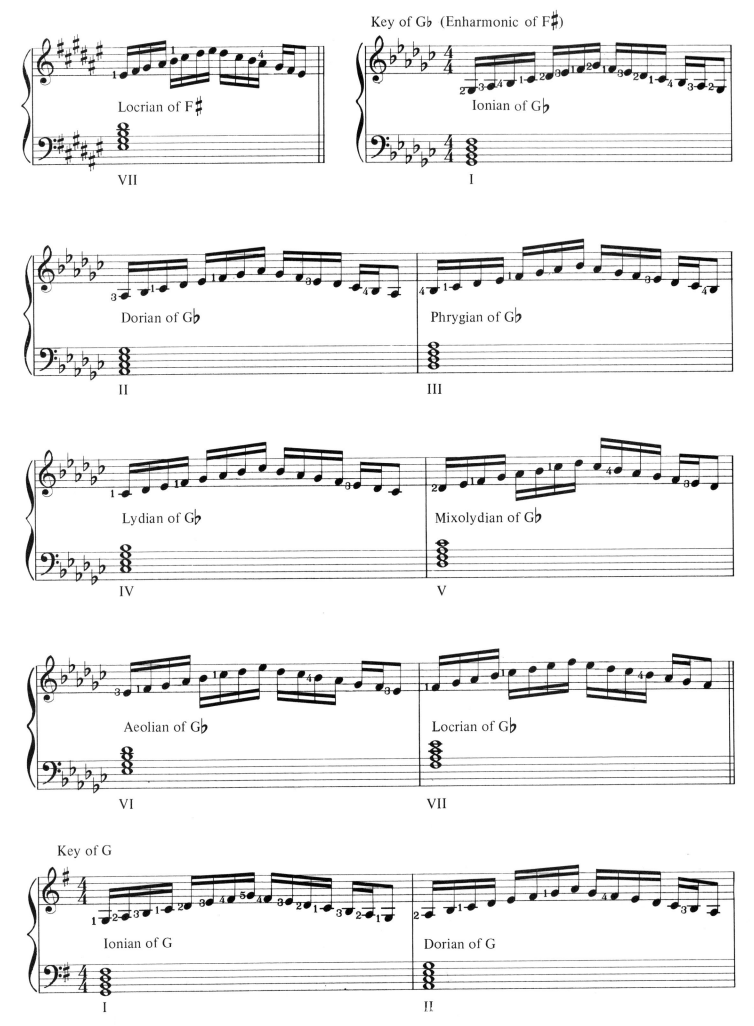

Key of G♭ (Enharmonic of F♯)

Locrian of F♯

VII

Ionian of G♭

I

Dorian of G♭

II

Phrygian of G♭

III

Lydian of G♭

IV

Mixolydian of G♭

V

Aeolian of G♭

VI

Locrian of G♭

VII

Key of G

Ionian of G

I

Dorian of G

II

68

Phrygian of G

III

Lydian of G

IV

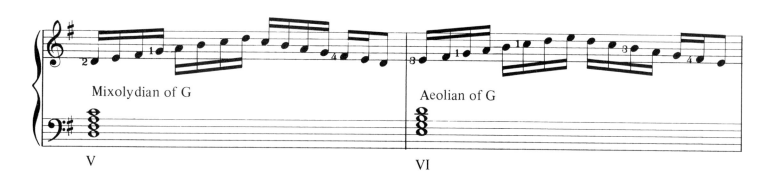

Mixolydian of G

V

Aeolian of G

VI

Locrian of G

VII

Key of A♭

Ionian of A♭

I

Dorian of A♭

II

Phrygian of A♭

III

Lydian of A♭

IV

Mixolydian of A♭

V

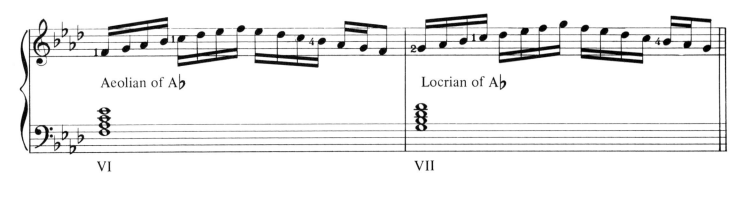

Aeolian of A♭ — VI

Locrian of A♭ — VII

Key of A

Ionian of A — I

Dorian of A — II

Phrygian of A — III

Lydian of A — IV

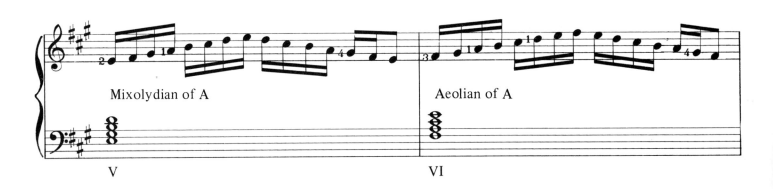

Mixolydian of A — V

Aeolian of A — VI

Locrian of A — VII

Key of B♭

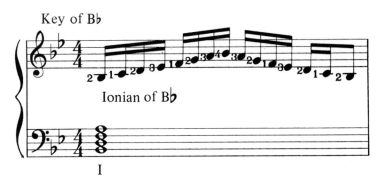

Ionian of B♭ — I

Dorian of B♭

II

Phrygian of B♭

III

Lydian of B♭

IV

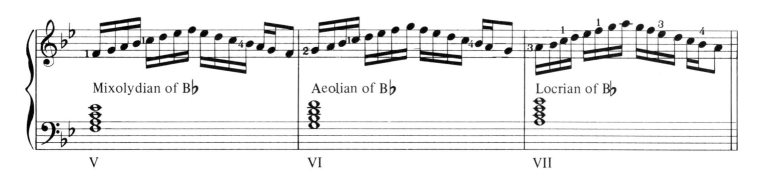

Mixolydian of B♭

V

Aeolian of B♭

VI

Locrian of B♭

VII

Key of B

Ionian of B

I

Dorian of B

II

Phrygian of B

III

Lydian of B

IV

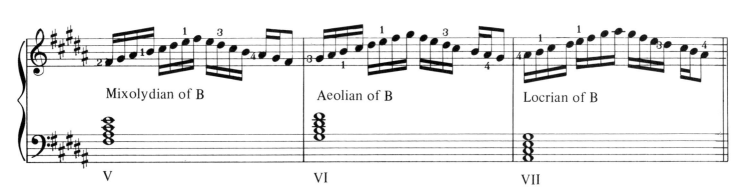

Mixolydian of B

V

Aeolian of B

VI

Locrian of B

VII

Chapter 17

Modal Improvisation (Part 1)

Until 1940 the basic element employed in jazz improvisation was the arpeggio (broken chord). This was evolved by Louis Armstrong, Coleman Hawkins and a host of other gifted performers. Beginning in the late Thirties with the appearance of Lester Young, Charlie Parker, Fats Navarro and Bud Powell the use of displaced scales (modes) began and has continued to dominate the improvised line to the present day.

Now we have to connect the modal system described in Chapter Sixteen to the seventh chord harmonic system described in Chapter Two.

Fig. 1 illustrates the seventh chord system and the possible modal relationships.

Fig. 1

Quality	Intervals	Positions	Modes
Major 7	M P M	I	Ionian
		IV	Lydian
Dominant 7th	M P m	V	Mixolydian
Minor 7th	m P m	II	Dorian
		III	Phrygian
		VI	Aeolian
Half diminished 7th	m o m	VII	Locrian
Diminished 7th	m o o	none	none

The Major 7th

I - Ionian
IV - Lydian

The problem with the major chord lies in the fact that I is always I, but IV may be IV or I of a new key. Eventually, the decision as to which of the two modes to choose will be left to the student;but,for an initial drill all majors will be treated as I taking the Ionian mode.
Fig. 2 illustrates the twelve major chords with their accompanying Ionian modes. These modes should be practiced first one octave, then two, both ascending and descending for complete automatic facility.

The Major Scales

Fig.2

CM   D♭M

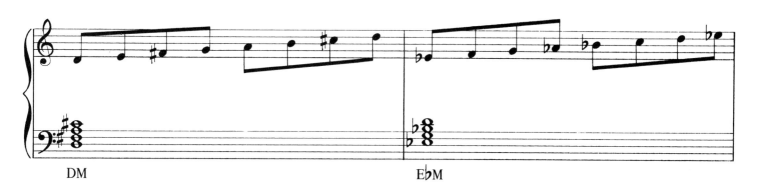

DM   E♭M

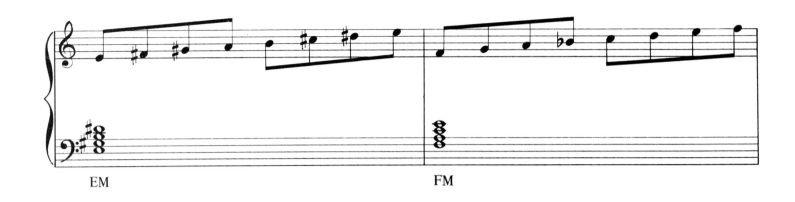

EM   FM

(Enharmonic)

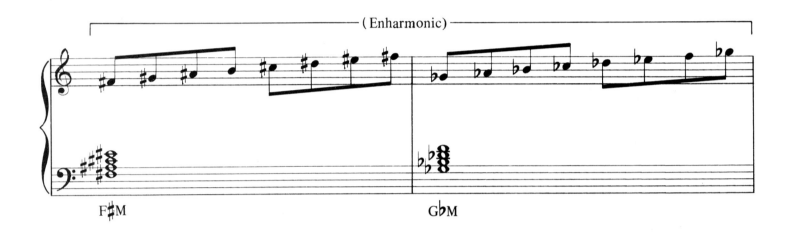

F♯M   G♭M

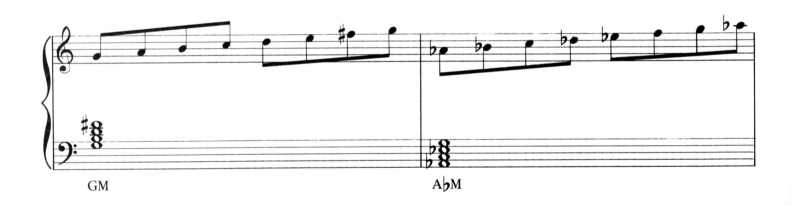

GM   A♭M

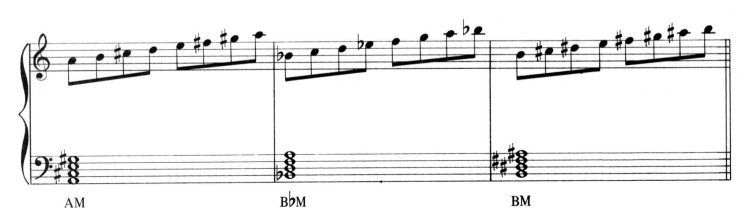

AM   B♭M   BM

The Dominant seventh

There is never any question about the status of the dominant chord since it only appears in the position of V. Fig. 3 illustrates the twelve dominant chords with their accompanying Mixolydian modes. These modes should be practiced first one octave, then two, both ascending and descending for complete automatic facility.

The Dominant Scales

Fig. 3

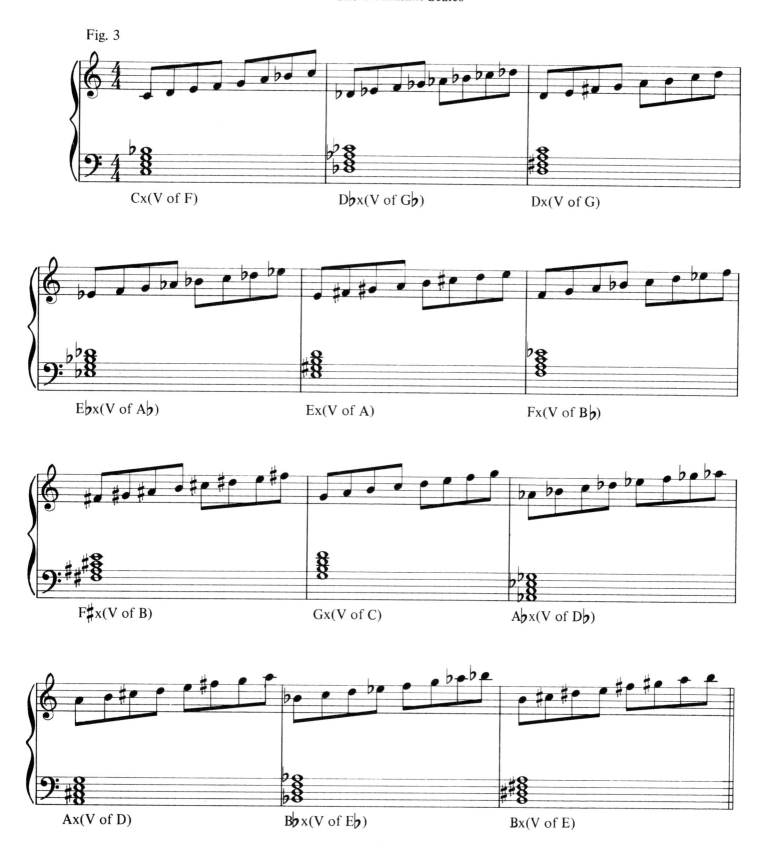

Cx(V of F)   Dbx(V of Gb)   Dx(V of G)

Ebx(V of Ab)   Ex(V of A)   Fx(V of Bb)

F#x(V of B)   Gx(V of C)   Abx(V of Db)

Ax(V of D)   Bbx(V of Eb)   Bx(V of E)

The Minor 7th.

II - Dorian
III - Phrygian
VI - Aeolian

The minor chord is the most difficult to deal with since it appears in three positions
(II - III - VI). For an initial drill the position of II (Dorian) will be used since the II
position is the most commonly employed. Also the II chord forms an integral part of
the basic cadence II - V - I (a basic anchor of all jazz improvisation). More advanced
decisions should be left to the individual choice of the student.

Fig. 4 illustrates the twelve minor chords with their accompanying Dorian modes. These
modes should be practiced first one octave, then two, both ascending and descending
for complete automatic facility.

The Minor Scales

Fig. 4

Cm(II of B♭)   C♯m(II of B)

Dm(II of C)   E♭m(II of D♭)

Em (II of D)   Fm (II of E♭)

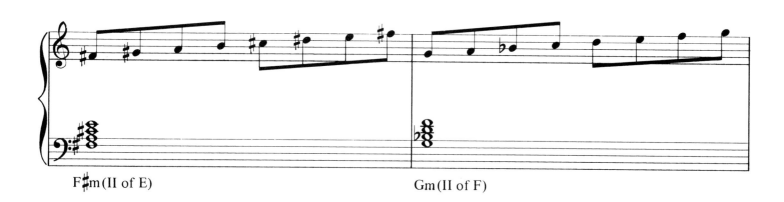

F♯m (II of E)   Gm (II of F)

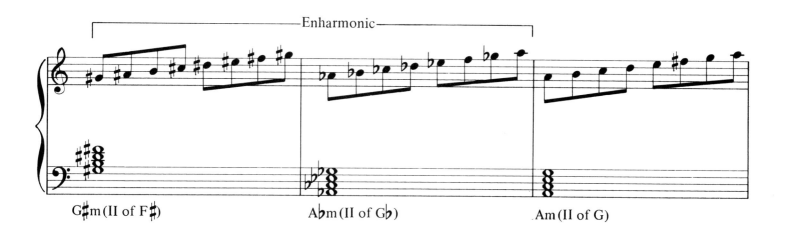

G♯m (II of F♯)   A♭m (II of G♭)   Am (II of G)

B♭m (II of A♭)   Bm (II of A)

The Half Diminished Chord

Like the dominant chord, the half diminished chord appears in only one position (VII) and therefore always employs the Locrian mode.

Fig. 5 illustrates the twelve half diminished chords with their accompanying Locrian modes. These modes should be practiced first one octave, then two, both ascending and descending for complete automatic facility.

The Half Diminished Scales

Fig. 5

C$^\emptyset$ (VII of D♭)   C♯$^\emptyset$ (VII of D)

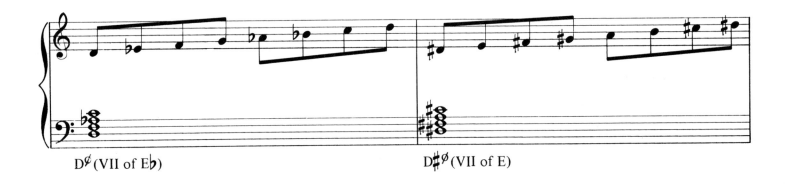

D$^\emptyset$ (VII of E♭)   D♯$^\emptyset$ (VII of E)

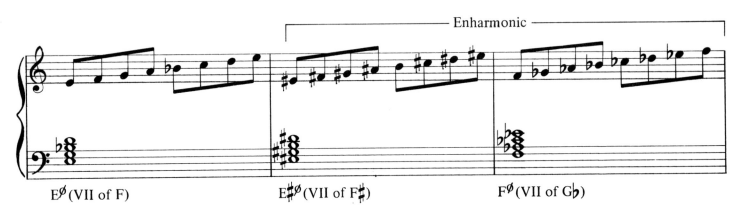

E$^\emptyset$ (VII of F)   E♯$^\emptyset$ (VII of F♯)   F$^\emptyset$ (VII of G♭)

F#ø (VII of G)   Gø (VII of Ab)

G#ø (VII of A)   Aø (VII of Bb)

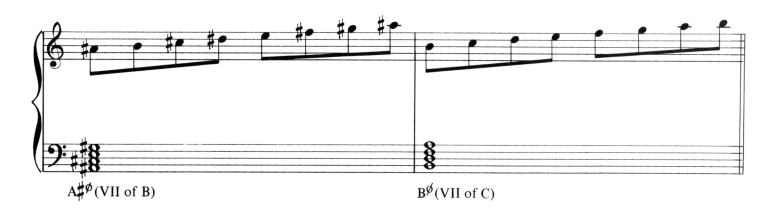

A#ø (VII of B)   Bø (VII of C)

The Diminished Chord

The diminished chord presents a special problem since it does not appear
naturally in the seventh chord system with which jazz is essentially concerned.
To overcome this problem, jazz musicians have evolved two artificial scales
which can be used interchangeably to accommodate the diminished chord.
The two scales employ alternating major and minor seconds.

The Diminished Scales

Fig.6 and 7 illustrate the two alternating scales.

Fig. 6 Semitone combination: 021212121

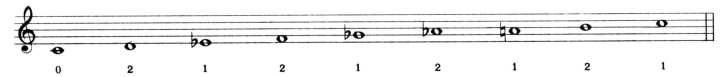

2 indicates two half steps; 1 indicates one half step.

Fig. 7 Semitone combination: 012121212

Fig. 8 illustrates the twelve 021212121 diminished scales. The numbers indicate suggested fingerings.

Fig. 8

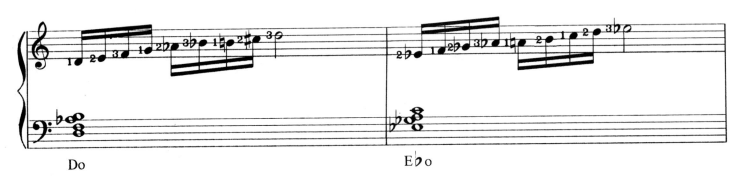

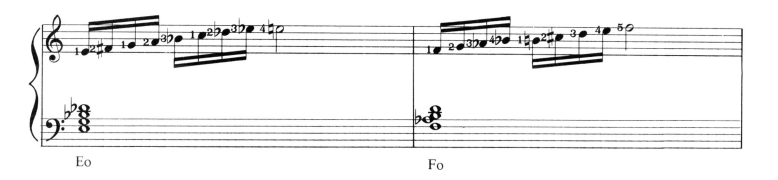

Eo

Fo

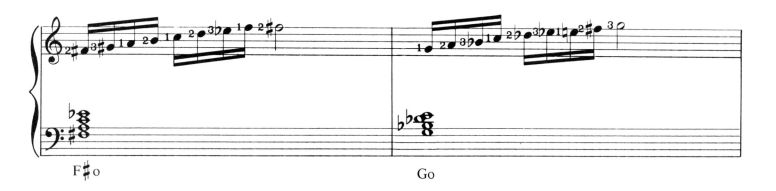

F♯o

Go

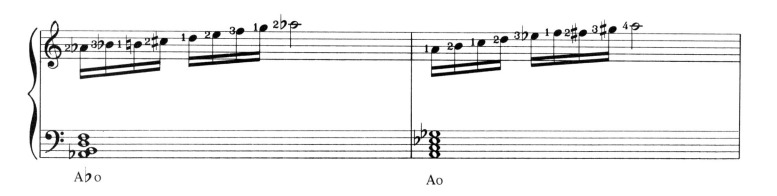

A♭o

Ao

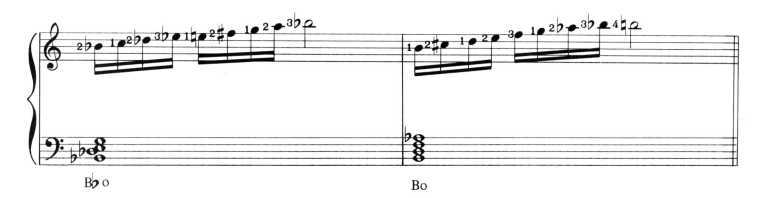

B♭o

Bo

Fig. 9 illustrates the twelve 012121212 diminished scales. The numbers indicate suggested fingerings.

Fig. 9

Co

C#o

Do

E♭o

Eo

Fo

F#o

Go

G#o

Ao

B♭o

Bo

82

Chapter 18

Modal Improvisation (Part 2)

To complete the modal system we must deal with the three modes (Phrygian, Lydian, Aeolian) that were temporarilly put aside in Chapter Seventeen.

The IV chord may be treated as IV or the I of a new key.
See Fig. 1

Fig. 1

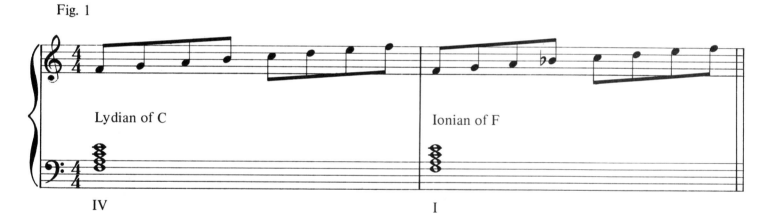

What determines the status of the IV chord is the preceding harmony.
In Fig. 2, the harmony is centered around the I chord so that IV would assume its natural role and take the Lydian mode.

Fig. 2

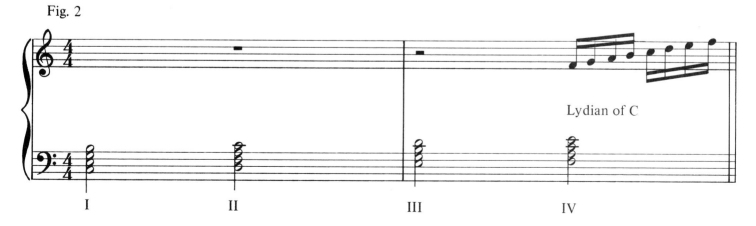

In Fig. 3, the key center around I has been weakened by the Vm and Ix and, as a result, the IV becomes the I of F.

As with all these modal conflicts, the student should make the decision concerning the "status" of the chord.

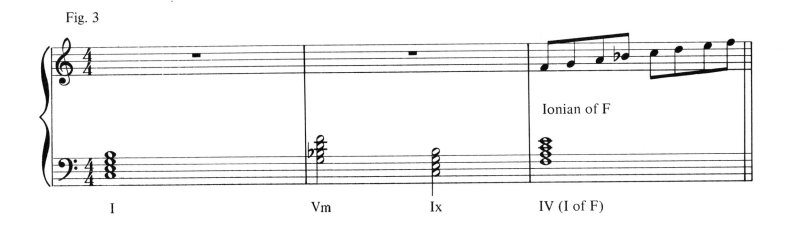

Fig. 3

The III chord and the VI chord may be the III or VI of the original key or the II of a new key.

In Fig. 4, the strong tonal center establishes III as III and VI as VI.

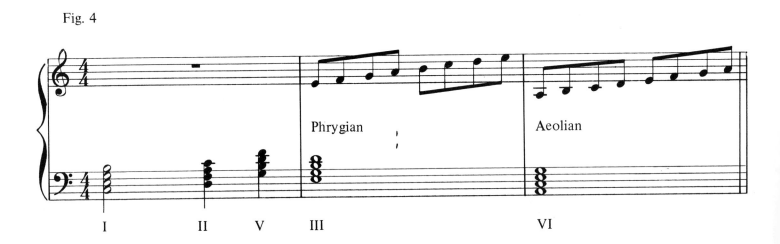

Fig. 4

In Fig. 5, the secondary functions in the case of III (IVm, ♭VIIx) and VI (VIIm, IIIx) establish the III as the II of D and the VI as the II of G.

Fig. 5

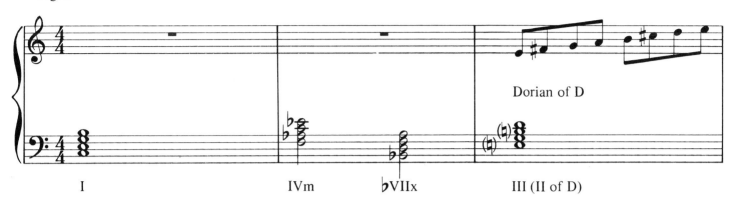

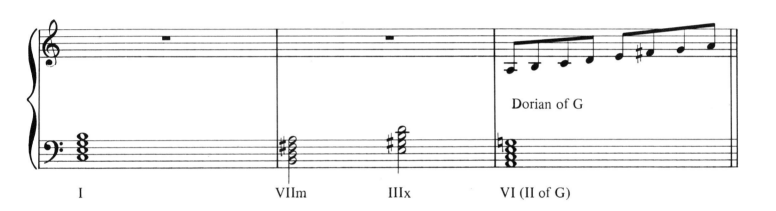

Fig. 6 illustrates the application of modal improvisation to "Polka Dots and Moonbeams" in the key of F. The III - IV and VI chords have been indicated as to status.

The bass line for Fig. 6 is as follows:

Introduction

(F) I VI / II ♭Vm VIIx // I VI/ IV II VIIm ♭VIIx/VI II♭$\frac{4}{3}$/VI$_2$ IV III♭III/

(F) II V VII$\frac{4}{3}$/III VI II V / I VI / II ♭Vm VIIx/

(F) I VI/ IV II VIIm ♭VIIx/ VI II♭$\frac{4}{3}$/ VI$_2$ IV III ♭III/

(F) II ♭IIx / I^{+6} (A) II∅ ♭IIx/I ♯Io/ II V /

(A) III VI / II ♭IIx / I ♯Io / II V //

(F) III VIx /II V / I VI / II ♭Vm VIIx /

(F) I VI/ IV II VIIm ♭VIIx/VI II♭ $\frac{4}{3}$ / VI$_2$ IV III ♭III /II ♭IIx / I //

85

Polka Dots and Moonbeams

Fig. 6 Key of F

words and music by
Johnny Burke and James Van Heusen

Introduction
Slowly

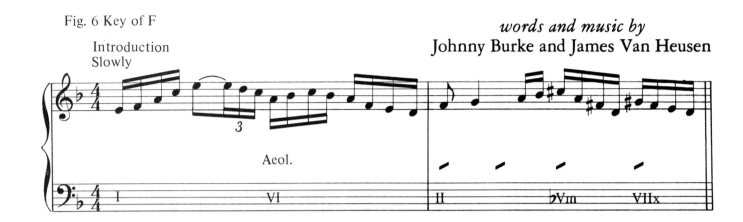

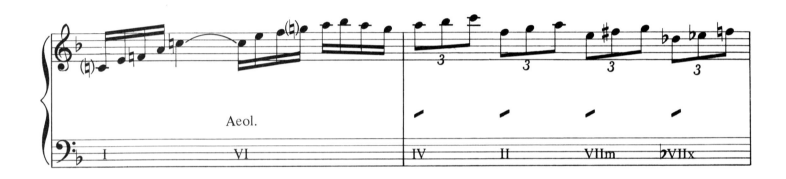

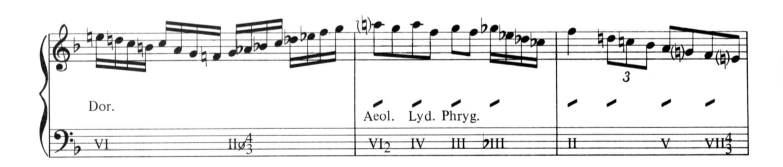

Chapter 19

The Non-modal Tones

The non - modal tones, often referred to as "blue notes", represent an
important element in jazz improvisation since the tension created by these
tones can add enormous excitement to a jazz performance.
It is often said that since Charlie Parker, there is no such thing as a "wrong"
note, only the performer's ability to make it sound "right". However, the
performer must keep a proper balance between the tension of the non -
modal tones and the release of the modal tones.
Fig 1. illustrates the non - modal or, in the case of the diminished scale,
non - scale tones relating to the five qualities.

Fig. 1   Modal Tones   Non - modal Tones

C major   C major

C dominant   C dominant

C minor (Dorian)   C minor

C half diminished   C half diminished

C diminished   C diminished

* The fourth step of both the major and dominant scales is often considered a tension tone unless the 3rd in the
  chord is raised to form an octave.

The non-modal tones in Fig. 1 break down into two categories

      1. Passing tones
      2. Ornamental tones

Passing tones	Ornamental tones
C major: C♯ D♯ A♯	F♯ = augmented 11th G♯ (if also raised in chord to form M7♯5)
C dominant: B	C♯ (D♭) = flatted 9th D♯ = augmented 9th F♯ = augmented 11th G♯ (A♭) = flatted 13th
C minor: C♯ E F♯ G♯ B	
C half diminished: E G A B	D = 9th
C diminished: C♯ E G B♭	

The use of ornamental tones in harmony will be thoroughly studied in a succeeding chapter. Fig. 2 illustrates the use of both passing tones and ornamental tones as they apply to the improvised line on "Bye Bye Baby". The following is the bass line for "Bye Bye Baby" in B♭.

```
                            ×7  ♯7
(B♭) I   Io/ I  ♯Io / II   II  / II    V  /

                            ×7      ♯7
(B♭) I   Io/ I  IV/ VIIm    VIIm / VIIm   IIIx   /

                      /  /  /    /   ×7  ♯7
(B♭) VI  ♭VIo / Vm  ♭V / IV  III  VIx / II   II  /

(B♭) II  ♭VIx / V   IVx / III  VIx  / II   V  /

                            ×7  ♯7
(B♭) I   Io  /I  ♯Io / II  II   / II    V  /

                              ×7     ♯7
(B♭) I   Io  / I   IV  / VIIm   VIIm  / VIm  IIIx /

(B♭) VI  ♭VIo / Vm  ♭V / IV   III  / II   ♯IIo  /

(B♭) III   VIx / II   V  / I    / I       //
```

Bye, Bye Baby

music by Jule Styne
words by Leo Robin

Fig. 2

(B♭) II   V   I   Io   I   ♯Io

(B♭) II   II   II   V   I   Io
      𝄪7   ♯7

(B♭) I   IV   VIIm   VIIm   VIm   IIIx
                        𝄪7   ♯7

(B♭) VI   ♭VIo   Vm   ♭V   IV   III

(B♭) II   ♯IIo   III   VIx   II   V   I   I

92

Chapter 20

Early Contemporary Left Hand Voicings

As was apparent in the transition from swing to bop piano (Chapters eleven and twelve) and again from bop to early contemporary (Chapters twelve and thirteen), revolutionary changes took place in the left hand structures employed in jazz piano.

Early contemporary left hand voicings began with two structures associated with classical piano. The earlier structure (referred to in this text as the (A) form) is usually attributed to Chopin and can be found extensively in his piano compositions. The more modern structure (referred to in this text as the (B) form) is usually attributed to the French impressionists, especially Maurice Ravel.

The following table describes the basic II-V-I procedure for the (A) form employing the Dorian, Mixolydian and Ionian modes.

II - 3572 - Dorian
V - 7236 - Mixolydian
I - 3562 - Ionian
See Fig. 1

The (A) Form

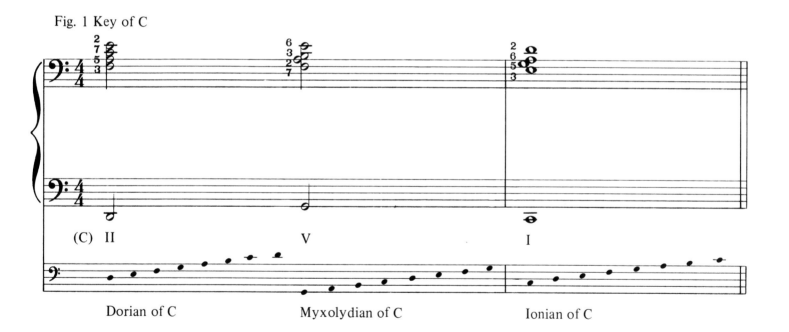

Fig. 1 Key of C

(C) II   V   I

Dorian of C   Myxolydian of C   Ionian of C

In the initial drill (Fig. 2), the voicings are played by the right hand in the middle C area; the root (which eventually would be assumed by the bass player in a group) is played by the left hand in the deeper range of the bass clef.

The II chord in each case creates a minor ninth chord; the V chord in each case creates a dominant nine thirteen chord; the I chord in each case creates a major ninth chord with an added sixth.

The (A) form will be studied in the keys of C, D♭, D, E♭, E and F. This is to ensure that the register of the voicings is always around middle C.

Fig. 2 Drill
Key of C

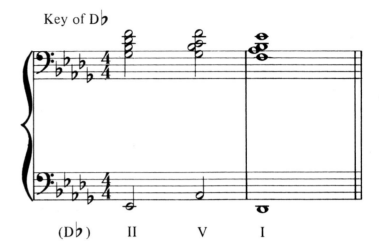

Key of Db

(C)   II   V   I

(Db)   II   V   I

Key of D

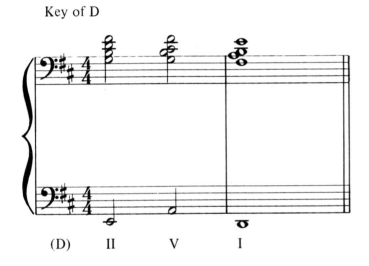

Key of Eb

(D)   II   V   I

(Eb)   II   V   I

Key of E

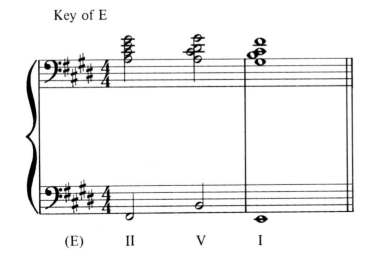

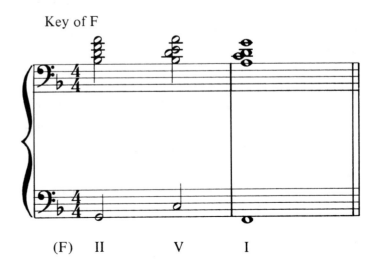

Key of F

(E)   II   V   I

(F)   II   V   I

The following table describes the basic II - V - I procedure for the Ⓑ form employing the Dorian, Mixolydian and Ionian modes.

II - 7 2 3 5 - Dorian

V - 3 13 7 2 - Mixolydian

I - 6 2 3 5 - Ionian

See Fig. 3

The Ⓑ Form

Fig. 3 Key of G

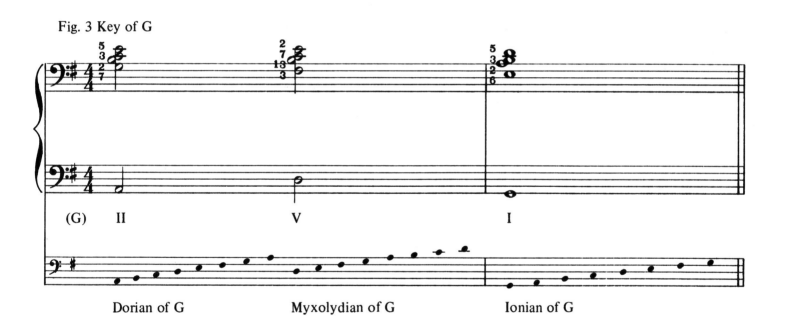

In the initial drill (Fig. 4), the Ⓑ form will be studied in the keys of G, A♭, A, B♭, B and F♯. This is to ensure that the register of the voicings is always around middle C.

Fig. 4 Drill
Key of G

(G)　II　　V　　I

Key of A♭

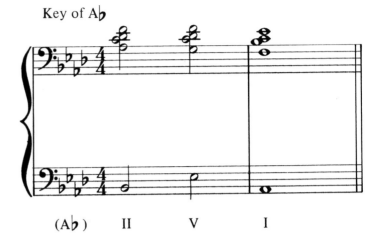

(A♭)　II　　V　　I

Key of A

(A)　II　　V　　I

Key of B♭

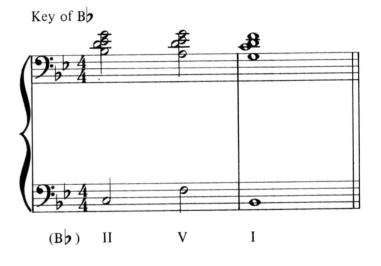

(B♭)　II　　V　　I

Key of B

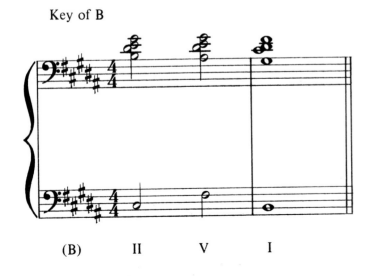

(B)　II　　V　　I

Key of F♯

(F♯)　II　　V　　I

The use of II - V - I is due to its elemental role in jazz improvisation. The problem now is to break open the II - V - I capsule in order to accommodate the Sixty Chord demands of jazz

Therefore:

All major chords are I
All dominant chords are V
All minor chords are II
All half diminished chords are II $^{\flat 5}$
All diminished chords are II $^{\flat 5}_{\flat 7}$ ⎤ See note

Note: In the case of half diminished and diminished chords, the voicings are derived from the chord (minor) with the most similar intervals to ∅ and o. (See Fig. 5)

Fig. 5 Key of C

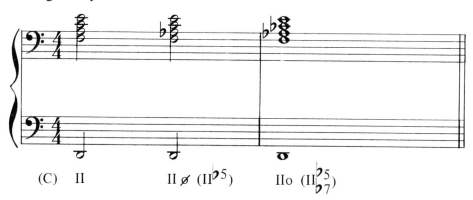

(C)   II   II ∅ (II $^{\flat 5}$)   IIo (II $^{\flat 5}_{\flat 7}$)

If the student attempts to play the Ⓐ form in the Ⓑ form keys or vice versa, it will be noticed immediately that the voicing is too low or too high and removed from the middle C area. To avoid this the following rule is applied:

If the parent key of the chord occurs between C and F (C, D♭, D, E♭, E, F), use the Ⓐ form ; if the parent key occurs between F♯ and B (F♯, G, A♭, A, B♭, B), use the Ⓑ form.

For example, VI in the key of C (a minor chord) becomes the temporary II of G and takes the Ⓑ form (G is a Ⓑ form key). On the other hand, VIx in the key of C (a dominant chord) is the temporary V of D and takes the Ⓐ form (D is an Ⓐ form key). (See Fig. 6)

Fig. 6 Key of C

(C)   VI (II of G)   VIx (V of D)   IVm (II of E♭) IVx (V of B♭)

The use of voicings in this manner automatically offers the student the following:

> Proper register (keyboard area)
> Proper voice - leading
> Automatic ornamentation
> Contemporary sound

Author's note; It is absolutely essential that the student memorize an automatic facility with the twelve II - V - I patterns in Figs. 2 and 4.

The Basic Theory of Intervals

Fig. 7

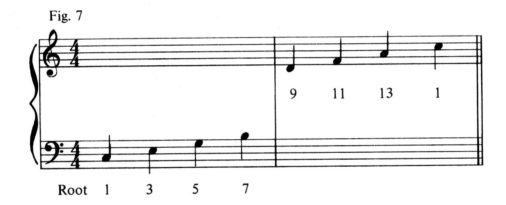

In Fig. 7 the basic theory of all intervals is illustrated.

Intervals are traditionally conceived in alternate steps with odd numbers (1, 3, 5, 7, etc.); however, when building structures, 9 can be identified for convenience as 2, 11 as 4 and 13 as 6; but these tones still retain their original status or function.

The exception to this is the sixth tone which, as the following table will indicate, takes on different values depending upon the quality of the particular chord.

The Sixth Tone:

> Major 7th chord = added 6th
> Dominant 7th chord = 13th
> Minor 7th chord = added 6th
> Half diminished 7th chord = non-functioning
> Diminished 7th chord = 7th of the chord

The unique quality of the 13th in the dominant chord results from the combination of the major 3rd and the minor 7th in the dominant chord.

Chapter 21

Contemporary Left Hand Voicings
Scales

Figures 1 through 13 illustrate the voicing system through the twelve major scales. Note that the II - V - I parent key system has been used in order to determine the (A) or (B) form status of each voicing.

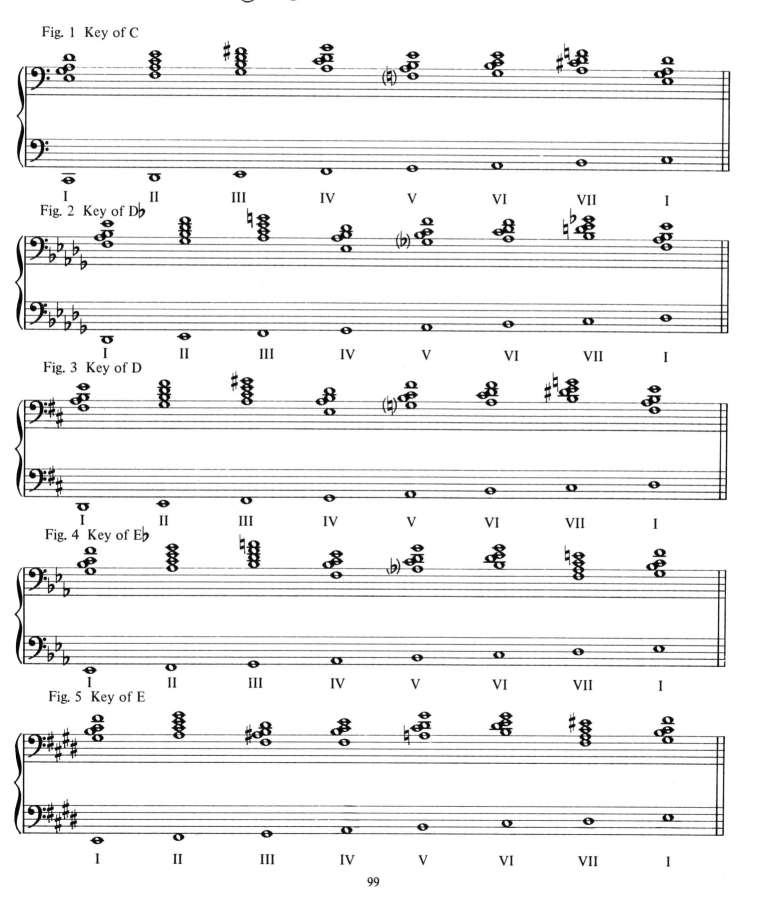

Fig. 6 Key of F

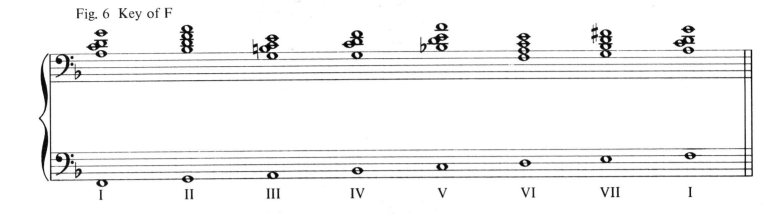

I II III IV V VI VII I

Fig. 7 Key of F♯
(Enharmonic of G♭)

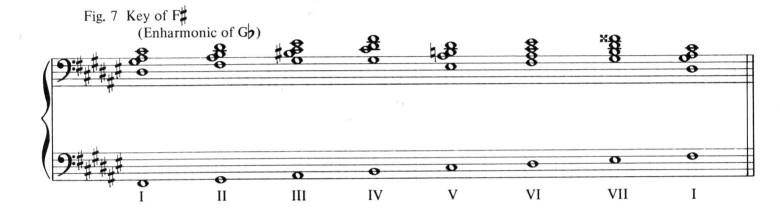

I II III IV V VI VII I

Fig. 8 Key of G♭
(Enharmonic of F♯)

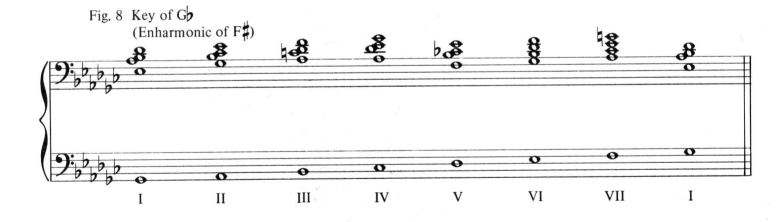

I II III IV V VI VII I

Fig. 9 Key of G

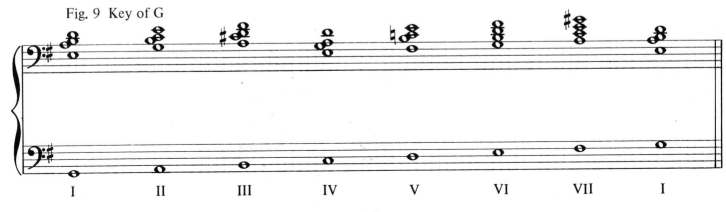

I II III IV V VI VII I

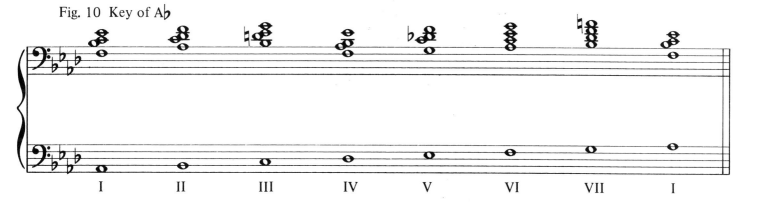

Fig. 10 Key of A♭

I II III IV V VI VII I

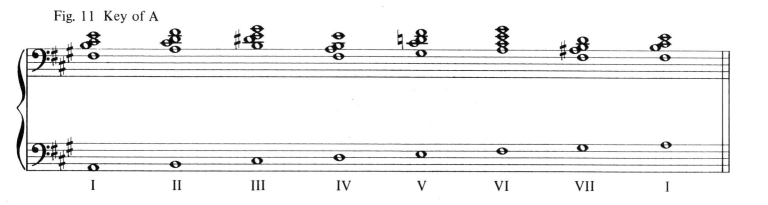

Fig. 11 Key of A

I II III IV V VI VII I

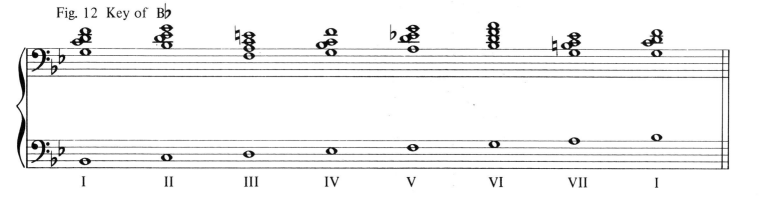

Fig. 12 Key of B♭

I II III IV V VI VII I

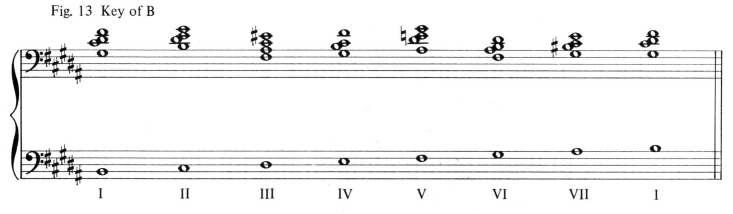

Fig. 13 Key of B

I II III IV V VI VII I

Chapter 22

Contemporary Left Hand Voicings
Five Qualities

Figures 1 through 12 illustrate the voicing system applied to the five chord qualities.

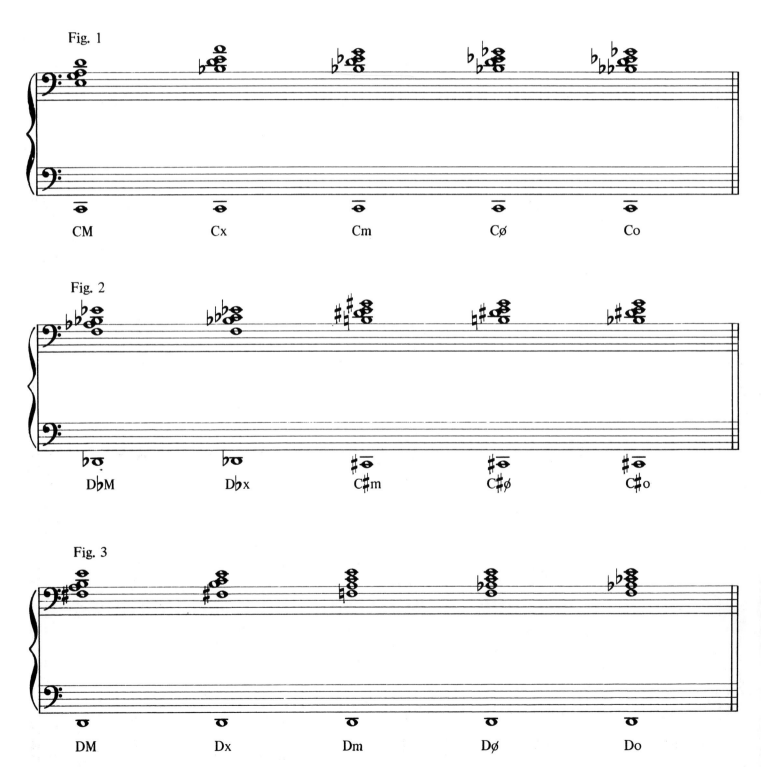

Fig. 1

CM   Cx   Cm   Cø   Co

Fig. 2

D♭M   D♭x   C♯m   C♯ø   C♯o

Fig. 3

DM   Dx   Dm   Dø   Do

Fig. 4

E♭M   E♭x   E♭m   E♭ø   E♭o

Fig. 5

EM   Ex   Em   Eø   Eo

Fig. 6

FM   Fx   Fm   Fø   Fo

Fig. 7

F♯M   F♯x   F♯m   F♯ø   F♯o

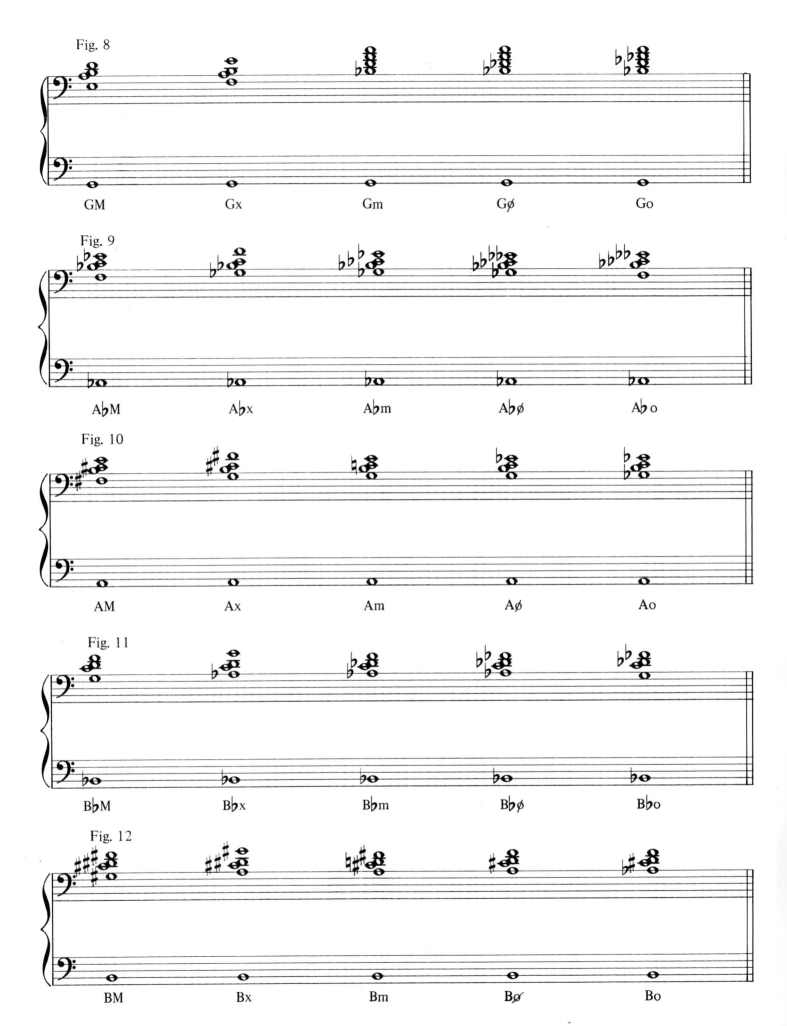